weekend
WOODWORKING VOL. 2 ™

Sawdust

One of the things I enjoy most about woodworking is mastering a new technique or picking up a tip for completing a routine task. Breaking away from familiar procedures is often the key to giving a project greater strength, adding unique visual interest, or simplifying an assembly.

The projects in this book aren't difficult or time-consuming to build, but they're loaded with tips and techniques. Whether it's assembling a quilt rack with attractive, traditional joinery or adding splines to the miter joints of kitchen storage containers, you'll learn techniques that you can use time and time again.

To help you succeed, everything you need to know is contained in the pages of this book. Just follow along, and you'll have beautiful and practical projects to show for your weekend in the shop!

Phil Huber
Editor, Woodsmith Magazine

This book is brought to you by the editors of Woodsmith® Magazine. To subscribe, visit www.Woodsmith.com

ISBN# 9798656213400
Weekend Woodworking Vol-2 is published by Active Interest Media, 2143 Grand Ave., Des Moines, IA 50312
Woodsmith is a registered trademark of Cruz Bay Publishing, Inc.
© Copyright 2016, Cruz Bay Publishing an Active Interest Media Company.
All rights reserved.
PRINTED IN THE USA

WEEKEND WOODWORKING

contents

storage solutions

6

home office

34

shop notebook

50

kitchen accessories

60

shop projects

78

Storage
Solutions

Some of the best projects are the ones that provide accessible storage for everyday items. Completely practical yet interesting to look at, these designs are sure to be family favorites.

Magazine Rack

This free-standing rack will keep your magazines neat and close at hand. It's simple to build with mortise and tenon joints.

Magazine racks are typically built for practical reasons — not to show off decorative joinery or fancy woods. And this rack is no different. I wanted an easily accessible place to keep magazines, and I wanted the design to be simple enough to complete in a weekend.

DESIGN FEATURES. Besides a clean design and simple construction, I also had a couple of other features in mind to make the rack as useful as possible.

For one thing, I wanted to make it easy to see what magazines or catalogs are there — without having to dig through a pile. That's why I came up with this open design. And I also wanted to be able to grab magazines comfortably while sitting, so I "lifted" the rack up off the floor to put them within easy reach.

To achieve these features without becoming too complicated, the X-shaped rack consists of two identical, interlocking frames (photo above). Each of these frames is built with basic mortise and tenon joinery, which creates a sturdy assembly that's quick to build.

LEGS & RAILS

As I just mentioned, to build this magazine rack, you essentially make two identical frames. You can see what I mean in the top drawing on the next page. Each frame starts out as two legs connected by two rails.

LEGS. I started by cutting the four legs to size from ¾"-thick stock. (The legs are 1¼" wide and 26⅛" long.)

The legs and rails will be assembled with mortise and tenon joints. I usually find it easiest to cut the mortises first and then size the tenons to fit. So the first thing to do is lay out the mortises on the legs.

The thing that's a bit odd here is that the two mortises on each leg aren't the same size. The reason for this is simple. The tenon on the top rail is offset, so there will be plenty of room to cut the curve along the top edge of the frame — without exposing the tenon.

To cut the mortises, start by clamping a fence to the drill press table. Then drill a series of ¼"-diameter, overlapping holes, as you see in Figure 1.

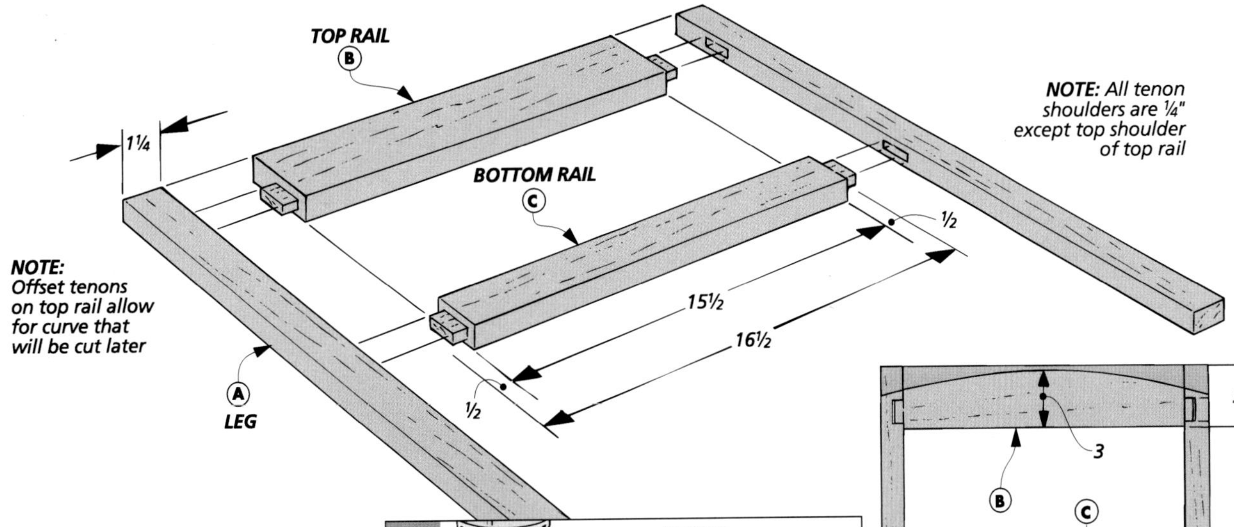
TOP RAIL
B
1¼
BOTTOM RAIL
C
NOTE: All tenon shoulders are ¼" except top shoulder of top rail
½
15½
16½
½
NOTE: Offset tenons on top rail allow for curve that will be cut later
A
LEG

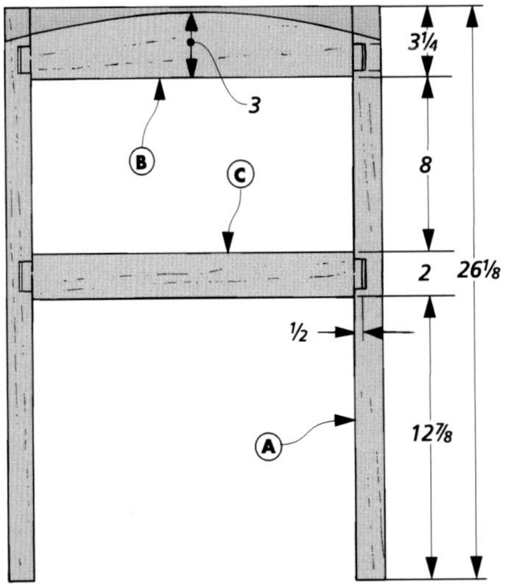
3¼
3
B
C
8
2
26⅛
½
A
12⅞

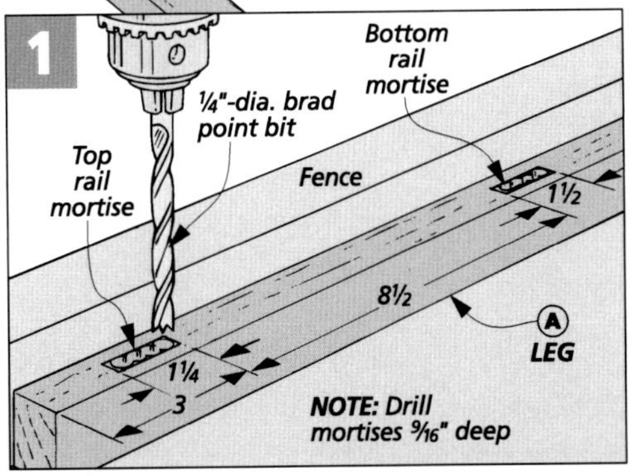
1
Bottom rail mortise
¼"-dia. brad point bit
Top rail mortise
Fence
1½
8½
A
LEG
1¼
3
NOTE: Drill mortises 9⁄16" deep

Here's a technique that I often use when drilling mortises: Set the bit to drill the mortises slightly deeper than the length of the tenons. (My mortises were drilled 9/16" deep.) This extra 1/16" creates a little bit of space for excess glue.

After the mortises are drilled, there's a little hand work to do. The sides of the mortises need to be cleaned up with a chisel. And the ends of the mortises need to be squared up to accept the tenons.

RAILS. With the mortises on the legs complete, work can begin on the top and bottom rails, as shown in the drawing at the top of the page. Both are cut to finished length (16½"), and the bottom rail is cut to finished width (2"). The only difference is the top rail starts off extra wide (3¼"). This allows for the curve on the top edge.

Once the rails are cut to size, the next step is to cut the ½"-long tenons on the ends of the rails (Figure 2). To do this, I used the table saw and made a series of passes over the blade. To make sure the shoulders of each tenon align, I clamped a short block to the rip fence to act as a stop.

It's important to size the tenons on the rails to fit the mortises in the legs. Almost all the shoulders here are the same. Mine were ¼" (Figure 2a). The only exception is the top shoulder on each top rail. To offset these shoulders, I raised the saw blade to 1¾" high (Figure 2b).

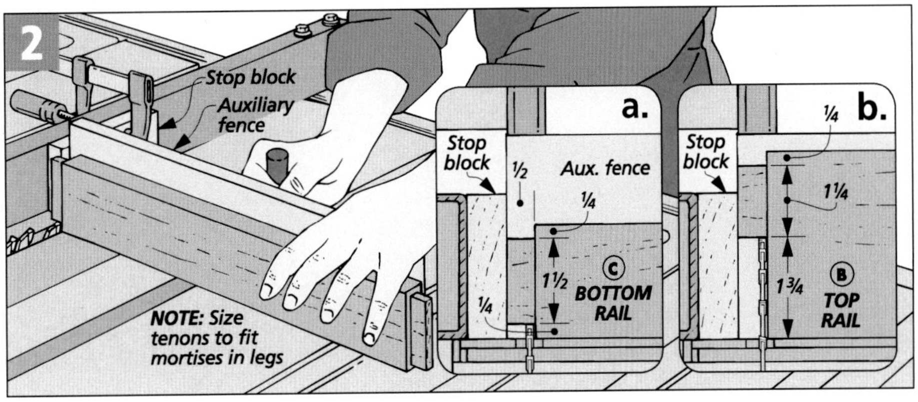
2
Stop block
Auxiliary fence
NOTE: Size tenons to fit mortises in legs
a.
Stop block
½
Aux. fence
¼
1½
C
BOTTOM RAIL
¼
b.
¼
Stop block
1¼
1¾
B
TOP RAIL

CUTTING DIAGRAM

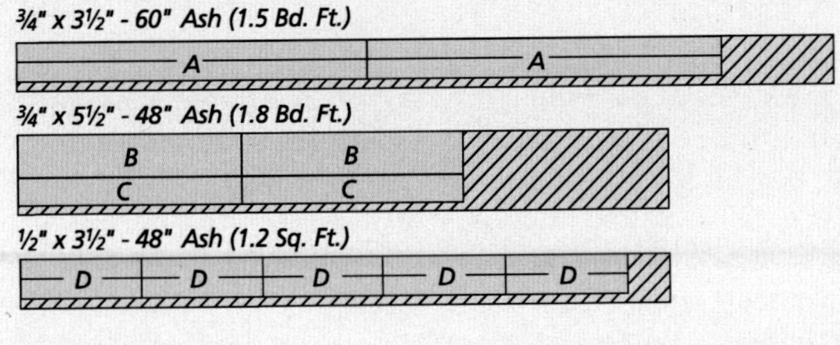
¾" x 3½" - 60" Ash (1.5 Bd. Ft.)
A
A
¾" x 5½" - 48" Ash (1.8 Bd. Ft.)
B
B
C
C
½" x 3½" - 48" Ash (1.2 Sq. Ft.)
D
D
D
D
D

MATERIALS

A	Legs (4)	¾ x 1¼ - 26⅛
B	Top Rails (2)	¾ x 3¼ - 16½
C	Btm. Rails (2)	¾ x 2 - 16½
D	Slats (10)	½ x 1½ - 9

Complete the Legs

With the mortises and tenons cut on the legs and rails, the next step is to dry assemble the frames (Figure 3). I had two goals in mind here. First, I wanted to check the fit of the frame. But more importantly, I wanted to lay out the notches on the legs.

These angled notches are the key to the two frames sliding together after they're assembled. They allow the frames to interlock at the center and give the rack its X-shape.

LAY OUT NOTCHES. Laying out the notches was a bit confusing at first. But with the frame dry assembled, it's easier to see where the notches should end up (Figure 3).

The top of each notch should be flush with the bottom edge of the bottom rail (Figure 3a). If the notch is below the bottom rail, there will be a gap between the two frames when they're put together. A very slight gap is okay, but if it's too wide, then the magazines will slide through and end up on the floor.

Next, I laid out the bottom of the notch, as well as the angles on the edges of the legs. These are really just rough guide lines. When it comes time to cut the notches, you'll want to sneak up on the cut and make sure you get a good fit.

CUTTING THE NOTCHES. Now that the notches are laid out, you can disassemble the frames and get your saw ready. There's not much to this. The miter gauge is angled 20°, and I added an auxiliary fence that extends across the blade. This provides better support and reduces the chance that the back edge of the notch will chip out.

All that's left is to set the blade height. Since these notches are really just angled half laps, the height of the blade should equal half the width of the legs (⅝" in my case).

To cut the notches, start near the top layout line, sneaking up on (but leaving) the line. Make multiple passes over the saw blade until you approach the bottom layout line. When you get near this line,

test the fit of the pieces between passes until the legs fit together.

BEVEL ENDS. With the notches cut, the next step is to bevel the end of each leg to sit flat on the floor (Figure 5). To do this, tilt the blade 35° and trim off the bottom of the

leg (Figure 5a). Make sure the bevel is cut in the opposite direction as the notch. Also, use a stop block so the legs end up the same length.

Finally, knock off the point of the bevel so it won't break off. An ⅛" chamfer does the trick (Figure 5b).

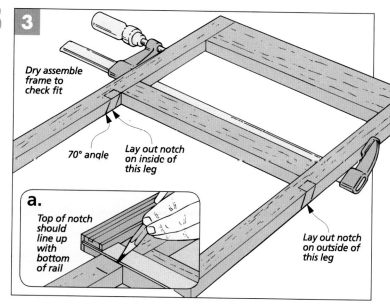

3

Dry assemble frame to check fit

70° angle

Lay out notch on inside of this leg

Lay out notch on outside of this leg

a. Top of notch should line up with bottom of rail

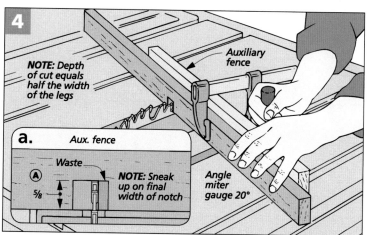

4

NOTE: Depth of cut equals half the width of the legs

Auxiliary fence

Angle miter gauge 20°

a. Aux. fence

Waste

Ⓐ ⅝

NOTE: Sneak up on final width of notch

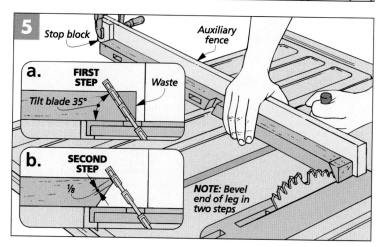

5

Stop block

Auxiliary fence

a. FIRST STEP

Tilt blade 35°

Waste

b. SECOND STEP

⅛

NOTE: Bevel end of leg in two steps

Slats & Assembly

Before you can assemble the frame, there's one last thing to do: Add the slats between the rails. Then the frame can be glued together and the curve can be cut on top.

CUT MORTISES. The first step to adding the slats is to cut the mortises in the top and bottom rails. Just like I did before, I used the drill press and cleaned up the mortises with a chisel. But what's important here is that all the mortises align. So, I carefully laid them out on one rail and then transferred the lines to the other rails with a square.

MAKE SLATS. With the mortises cut, I made the slats, as shown in the upper right illustration. These pieces are ½" thick and 1½" wide. The length of the slats depends on the distance between the rails. So to determine the length, I dry assembled a frame so I could measure the distance between the rails. This equals the shoulder-to-shoulder length of the slats. Then I simply cut them 1" longer for the ½"-long tenons. (My slats were 9" long.)

Once that's done, the next step is to cut tenons on both ends of each slat, as you can see in Figures 6 and 6a. Here again, I used a stop block clamped to the rip fence to establish the length of the tenons.

CREATE ARCS. After the tenons are cut, the frames can be glued together. Then when the glue is dry, all that's left is to create the arc on the top of each frame (Figure 7).

To do this, I drove a brad on each side of the frame. Then I bent a piece of ⅛" hardboard between the two nails so the rail was 3" wide at the center, as shown in Figure 7a.

With the arcs laid out on both of the top rails, I roughed them out with the band saw, staying about ¹⁄₁₆" on the waste side of the line. Then I sanded up to the line.

Finally, before sliding the two frames together, I used a ½" roundover bit to rout a decorative bullnose profile along the top edges, as you can see in Figure 8.

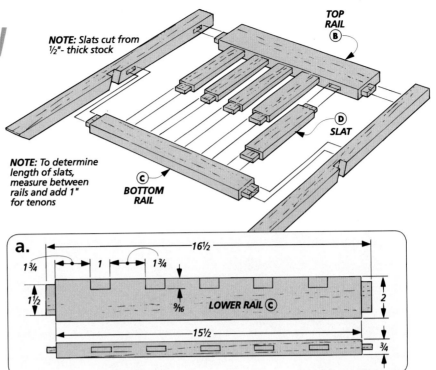

NOTE: Slats cut from ½"- thick stock

TOP RAIL (B)

(D) SLAT

NOTE: To determine length of slats, measure between rails and add 1" for tenons

(C)
BOTTOM RAIL

a. LOWER RAIL (C)
16½
1¾ 1 1¾
1½
9⁄16
2
15½
¾

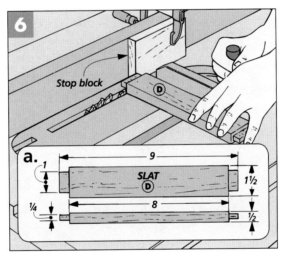

6 Stop block (D)

a. 9
1
SLAT (D)
1½
¼
8
½

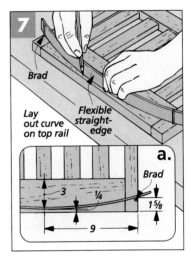

7 Brad
Lay out curve on top rail
Flexible straight-edge

a. Brad
3 ¼ 1⅝
9

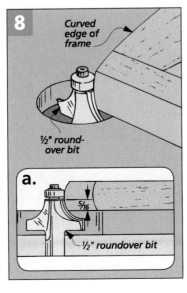

8 Curved edge of frame
½" round-over bit

a. 5⁄16
½" roundover bit

Tilt frames and slide them together

NOTE: Frames can be joined permanently with a spot of glue

DVD Storage Case

Organize your DVD collection in style with this easy-to-build case. It's versatile enough to work in any space, with any number of DVDs.

It doesn't take long to build up a rather sizable collection of DVDs. But the challenge is keeping them all organized and neatly stored. One of the reasons I like the DVD storage case you see in the photo above is because it solves that problem.

Another is that it's easy to build. The few joints you need to make can all be done at the router table.

The final thing that makes this project appealing is the design of the case. You can set the case horizontally (photo above) and stack a couple together so they'll look like an old library card catalog. Or you can stand a single case on end (photo at right) where it resembles a miniature filing cabinet.

Regardless of its position, the drawers slip in place smoothly. And your collection stays organized so you'll always be able to find the DVD you're looking for.

Stand It Upright. The storage case works just as well vertically. After standing it on end, simply give the drawers a quarter turn, and then slide them back in place.

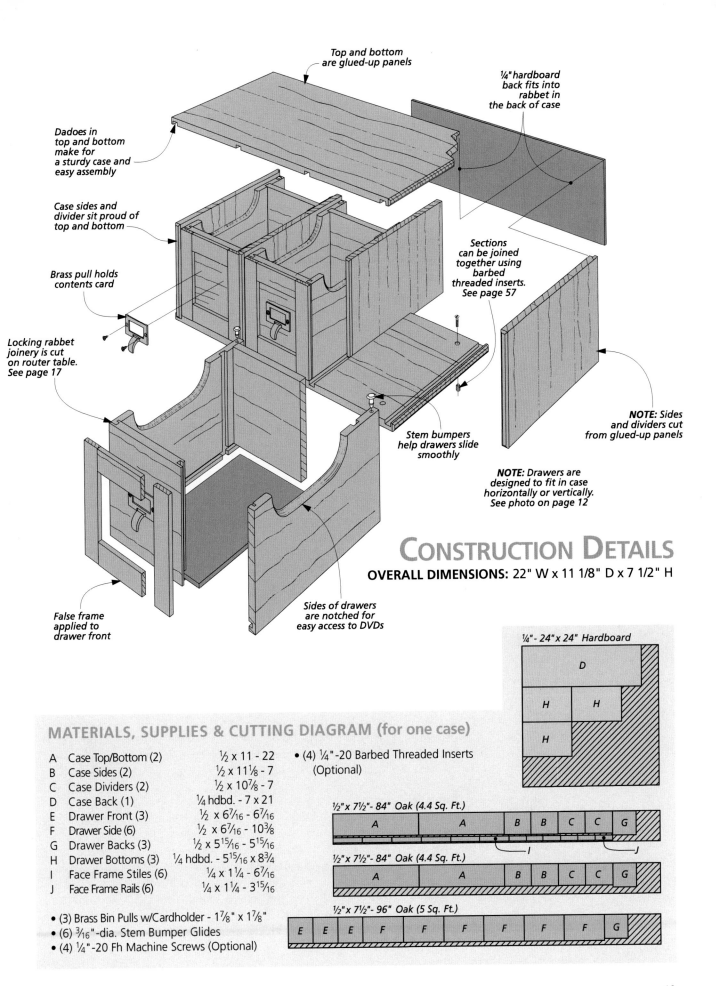

Top and bottom are glued-up panels

¼" hardboard back fits into rabbet in the back of case

Dadoes in top and bottom make for a sturdy case and easy assembly

Case sides and divider sit proud of top and bottom

Brass pull holds contents card

Sections can be joined together using barbed threaded inserts. See page 57

Locking rabbet joinery is cut on router table. See page 17

NOTE: Sides and dividers cut from glued-up panels

Stem bumpers help drawers slide smoothly

NOTE: Drawers are designed to fit in case horizontally or vertically. See photo on page 12

False frame applied to drawer front

Sides of drawers are notched for easy access to DVDs

CONSTRUCTION DETAILS
OVERALL DIMENSIONS: 22" W x 11 1/8" D x 7 1/2" H

¼" - 24" x 24" Hardboard

MATERIALS, SUPPLIES & CUTTING DIAGRAM (for one case)

A	Case Top/Bottom (2)	½ x 11 - 22
B	Case Sides (2)	½ x 11⅛ - 7
C	Case Dividers (2)	½ x 10⅞ - 7
D	Case Back (1)	¼ hdbd. - 7 x 21
E	Drawer Front (3)	½ x 6⁷⁄₁₆ - 6⁷⁄₁₆
F	Drawer Side (6)	½ x 6⁷⁄₁₆ - 10⅜
G	Drawer Backs (3)	½ x 5¹⁵⁄₁₆ - 5¹⁵⁄₁₆
H	Drawer Bottoms (3)	¼ hdbd. - 5¹⁵⁄₁₆ x 8¾
I	Face Frame Stiles (6)	¼ x 1¼ - 6⁷⁄₁₆
J	Face Frame Rails (6)	¼ x 1¼ - 3¹⁵⁄₁₆

- (4) ¼"-20 Barbed Threaded Inserts (Optional)

- (3) Brass Bin Pulls w/Cardholder - 1⅞" x 1⅞"
- (6) ³⁄₁₆"-dia. Stem Bumper Glides
- (4) ¼"-20 Fh Machine Screws (Optional)

½"x 7½"- 84" Oak (4.4 Sq. Ft.)

| A | A | B | B | C | C | G |

½"x 7½"- 84" Oak (4.4 Sq. Ft.)

| A | A | B | B | C | C | G |

½"x 7½"- 96" Oak (5 Sq. Ft.)

| E | E | E | F | F | F | F | F | F | G |

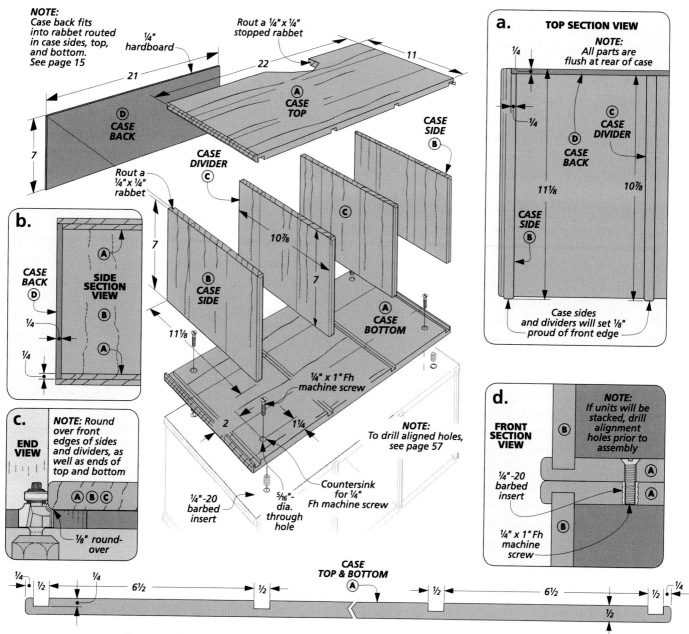

NOTE:
Case back fits into rabbet routed in case sides, top, and bottom. See page 15

1/4" hardboard

Rout a 1/4" x 1/4" stopped rabbet

21

22

11

7

D CASE BACK

A CASE TOP

B CASE SIDE

Rout a 1/4" x 1/4" rabbet

CASE DIVIDER **C**

C

C

7

10⅞

7

b.

CASE BACK **D**

SIDE SECTION VIEW

A

B

B CASE SIDE

A

1/4"

1/4"

11⅛

A CASE BOTTOM

1/4" x 1"Fh machine screw

a. TOP SECTION VIEW

NOTE: All parts are flush at rear of case

1/4

1/4

C CASE DIVIDER

D CASE BACK

11⅛

10⅞

CASE SIDE **B**

Case sides and dividers will set 1/8" proud of front edge

c.

END VIEW

NOTE: Round over front edges of sides and dividers, as well as ends of top and bottom

A B C

1/8" round-over

2

1¼

1/4" x 1"Fh machine screw

NOTE: To drill aligned holes, see page 57

1/4"-20 barbed insert

5/16"-dia. through hole

Countersink for 1/4" Fh machine screw

d.

FRONT SECTION VIEW

NOTE: If units will be stacked, drill alignment holes prior to assembly

B

1/4"-20 barbed insert

A

A

B

1/4" x 1"Fh machine screw

CASE TOP & BOTTOM **A**

1/4 · 1/2   1/4   6½   1/2   1/2   1/2   6½   1/2 · 1/4

1/2

Making the Case

As you see in the drawing above, the storage case is just a box with a couple of dividers. The key to making the box is creating perfectly square openings so the drawers will fit the case whether it's sitting horizontally or vertically.

To do this, I started by cutting the top and bottom to final size and then headed to the router table. The router is the best choice for making the dadoes that the sides and dividers of the case will fit into.

Since you'll see the dado at the front of the case, use a straight bit to cut a smooth, clean bottom and

create a tight-fitting joint. The next page shows you how this is done.

STOPPED RABBETS. While you're at the router table, you'll want to rout a rabbet along the back edge of both the top and bottom. It's sized to accept the back of the case (detail 'b'). Just be sure to start and stop the rabbet without routing through the ends of the top and bottom.

At this point, you can set the top and bottom aside and work on the case sides and dividers. Note that the sides are a 1/4" wider. This allows for the rabbet along the back edge to hold the back of the case (detail 'a').

And both the sides and dividers are sized to project slightly past the front edge of the top and bottom.

You're just about ready to assemble the case. But first, ease the sharp edges by routing or sanding a small roundover on the front edges of the sides and dividers, as well as the ends of the top and bottom (detail 'c' and the opposite page).

Finally, if you're building multiple cases, detail 'd' and a tip on page 57 show you the steps to take to join them together. Once that's complete, you can glue up the case and install the hardboard back.

Router Joinery

As I mentioned earlier, I used dadoes to join the case sides and dividers to the top and bottom. Since this joint will be "front and center," it's very important to cut perfectly smooth, flat, and chipout-free dadoes. To do this, I used my router table and a ½" straight bit, as you see in the photo at right.

ROUTING THE DADOES. The key to making the drawer compartments of the case identical in size is cutting evenly spaced and matched dadoes in both the top and bottom.

All it takes are a couple of simple steps, like you see in Figure 1. Start by routing the dadoes for the dividers. To do this, position the fence so it's 7¼" away from the bit. Then set the router bit to cut ¼" deep.

To prevent chipout as you complete the cut, use a backer board to push the workpiece over the bit, as you see at right. After completing the first cut, rotate the workpiece end for end and rout the dado for the second divider. Repeat the process on the bottom of the case.

The next step is to rout the dadoes at the ends. What's important here is to reset the fence so that after routing the two dadoes, the spacing between all of them is identical. In my case, I reset the fence ¼" from the bit.

ROUTING STOPPED RABBETS. You'll also need to make a couple of rabbets to hold the back of the case. If you look closely, you'll notice the rabbets are "stopped." That's so they aren't visible on the sides of the case. To make these cuts, you'll want to switch to a ¼" straight bit.

To match the depth of cut, you can use one of the dadoes you just routed as a setup gauge (Figure 2). I found it easiest to align the workpiece over the bit and then "drop" it down to begin the cut (Figure 3). Just be sure to stop the cut when you reach the dado that's at the end of the workpiece.

Finally, rout or sand a roundover to ease the edges (Figures 4 and 5).

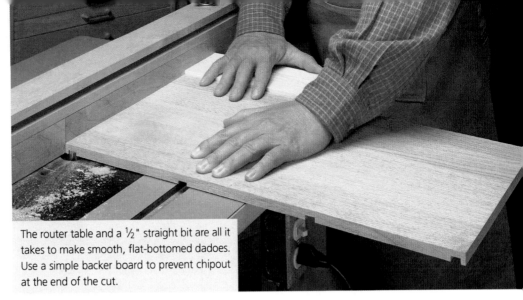

The router table and a ½" straight bit are all it takes to make smooth, flat-bottomed dadoes. Use a simple backer board to prevent chipout at the end of the cut.

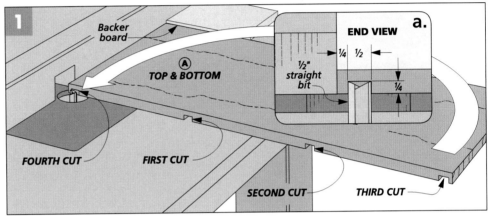

The first step in cutting the dadoes is to set the fence to cut the dadoes for the dividers. After you rout one dado, flip the workpiece end for end and make a second pass. Then you can reset the fence to space the dadoes evenly, as shown in detail 'a,' and rout the dadoes for the sides.

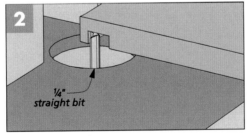

After installing a ¼" bit in the router, you can use one of the dadoes you just routed as a setup gauge for setting the depth of cut for the rabbet.

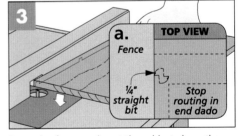

Reset the fence and rout the rabbet along the back edge of the top and bottom. Stop the cut when you reach the end dado (detail 'a').

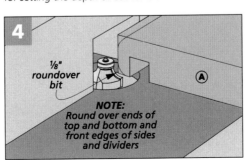

After routing the dadoes and rabbets, switch to a ⅛" roundover bit to soften the visible ends of the case top, bottom, sides, and dividers.

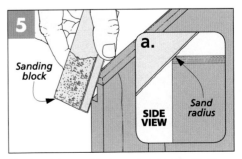

It's almost impossible to rout a roundover on the small ends of each piece. So it's best to switch to fine sandpaper and a sanding block.

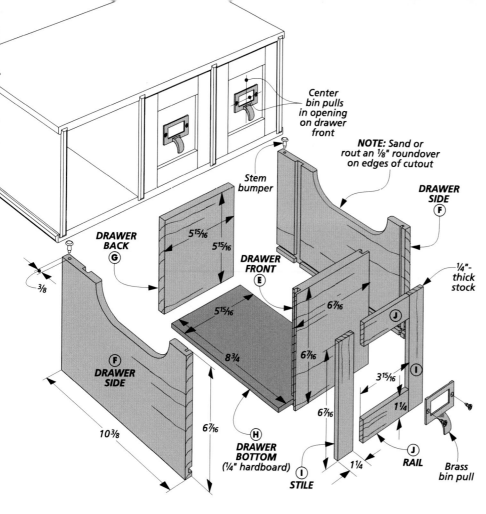

Center bin pulls in opening on drawer front

NOTE: Sand or rout an ⅛" roundover on edges of cutout

Stem bumper

DRAWER SIDE (F)

DRAWER BACK (G)

5¹⁵⁄₁₆
5¹⁵⁄₁₆

DRAWER FRONT (E)

¼"-thick stock

⅜

DRAWER SIDE (F)

5¹⁵⁄₁₆

6⁷⁄₁₆

6⁷⁄₁₆

(J)

8¾

6⁷⁄₁₆

3¹⁵⁄₁₆

(I)

DRAWER SIDE (F)

1¼

(J) RAIL

Brass bin pull

10⅜

6⁷⁄₁₆

6⁷⁄₁₆

(H)

DRAWER BOTTOM (¼" hardboard) (I) STILE

1¼

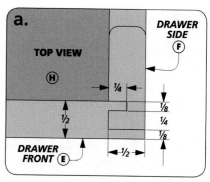

a. TOP VIEW (H)

DRAWER SIDE (F)

½

¼

⅛
¼
⅛

DRAWER FRONT (E)

½

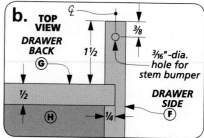

b. TOP VIEW

DRAWER BACK (G)

1½

⅜

³⁄₁₆"-dia. hole for stem bumper

DRAWER SIDE (F)

½

(H)

¼

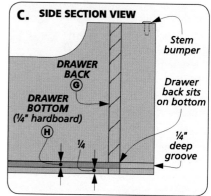

c. SIDE SECTION VIEW

Stem bumper

DRAWER BACK (G)

Drawer back sits on bottom

DRAWER BOTTOM (¼" hardboard) (H)

¼

¼" deep groove

Two-Way Drawers

With the case complete, you're ready to turn your attention to the drawers. The challenge is to build them to match the openings in the case so they fit whether the case is set horizontally or vertically.

DRAWER DETAILS. The drawers are built to have a small ¹⁄₁₆" clearance side to side and top to bottom. And the back of each drawer is recessed just a bit (drawing above). This way you can pull out a drawer and easily access the DVDs without

the drawer falling out of the case. Finally, to dress up the fronts of the drawers, I decided to add a miniature hardwood face frame.

FRONTS & SIDES. Since the front of the drawer determines its overall fit, I started by cutting each drawer front to fit an opening, allowing enough for the ¹⁄₁₆" clearance.

While I was at it, I cut the side pieces to the same width and trimmed them to final length. Then, to make it easy to reach a DVD in

the drawer, I made a cutout along the top edge of each side (drawing above and pattern below).

ROUTING A LOCKING RABBET JOINT. To join the fronts and sides, I used a locking rabbet joint, as shown in detail 'a' and on the opposite page

ADDING THE BACK & BOTTOM. Once the locking rabbet joints are cut, you're ready to add the back and bottom. The back fits into dadoes cut in each side piece (detail 'b'), and the bottom fits into grooves cut in the front and sides (detail 'c'). After cutting the pieces to size, you can glue up the drawer.

FINISH IT OFF. To give each drawer a finished look, I created a face frame by gluing thin strips of hardwood on the drawer fronts (drawing above). Finally, I added some plastic bumpers and a brass bin pull.

Now all that's left to do is round up your DVD collection, organize them, and slip them in place.

DRAWER CUTOUT PATTERN

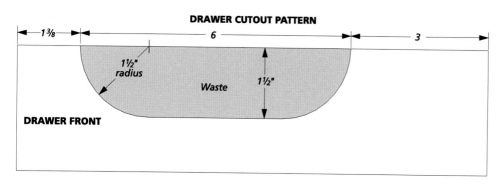

1⅜
6
3

1½" radius

Waste

1½"

DRAWER FRONT

Locking Rabbet

Even though the drawers of the DVD case are small, they're sure to get a lot of wear and tear. So to make sure they stand the test of time, I used a locking rabbet joint to attach the front to the sides.

START WITH A CENTERED GROOVE. Detail drawing 'a' on the opposite page shows you what an assembled locking rabbet joint looks like. This may look like a challenge at first. But you can complete this joint with just a few simple steps.

The first thing you'll need to do is cut a centered groove on each end of the drawer front. You can see how I did this in the photo and Figure 1 at right. But there are a few things I should point out.

First, I used a ¼" straight bit and set the bit to cut the full depth. Then, using an auxiliary table, you can cut the groove in two passes.

To do this, you'll want to be sure you have the fence set to center the groove perfectly. This is where some test pieces can really help you out. By making a few practice cuts and adjusting the fence, you'll be able to quickly center the groove.

I wanted to be sure I made a clean cut at both ends of the groove. So I used a backer board to support the workpiece. This eliminates the chance of any chipout as the router bit exits the end of the workpiece.

Now, go ahead and make the cuts on all the drawer fronts.

TRIMMING THE TONGUE. After making the grooves, you'll need to trim away part of the drawer front to create a tongue. This tongue fits the dado you'll be cutting in the side of the drawer. In Figure 2, you can see how I used the ¼" straight bit to trim the tongue to final length.

COMPLETING THE JOINT. All that's left to complete the locking rabbet joint is to cut a narrow dado in each drawer side to mate with the tongue. For this you'll need to switch to an ⅛" straight bit. Figure 3 covers the setup you'll need to get the fit of the tongue just right.

The router table and a few small straight bits make quick work of cutting a locking rabbet joint.

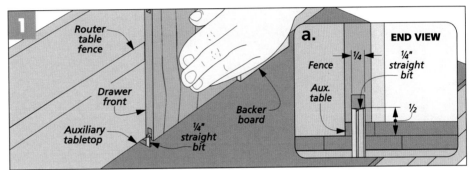

To center a groove in the ends of the drawer front, use a ¼" straight bit on the router table and set the depth to make a full ½"-deep cut.

Next, add an auxiliary table and adjust the fence. Make one pass, remove the auxiliary table, and then make a second pass.

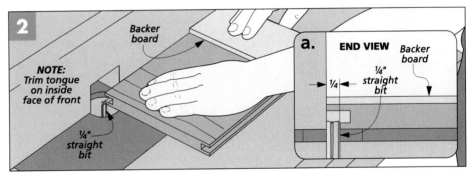

Next, you'll need to trim the end of the drawer front to create a small tongue. To do this in a single pass, I used the ¼" straight bit already installed in my router and the setup shown in detail 'a.' Here again, a backer board prevents the back edge from chipping out.

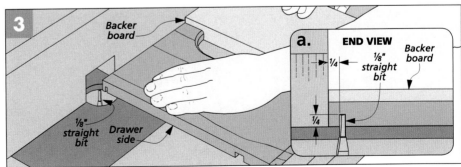

All that's left to complete the locking rabbet joint is to cut a narrow dado in each side piece to match the tongue on the drawer front. For this you'll need to install an ⅛" straight bit and make a single pass. Detail 'a' shows you the setup you'll need for doing this.

Drop-Front Storage Center

With storage above, below, and inside, this simple project allows you to organize all the items you never seem to have a place for.

Concealed Storage. The false-drawer front drops down to reveal storage for small items, while the double hooks provide a good place to hang coats, scarves, and hats.

At first glance, this storage center appears to have four small drawers to go with its four coat hooks. But a closer look reveals that these "drawers" aren't really drawers at all. As the photo on the left shows, they disguise a drop-front door that hides plenty of storage for hats, sunglasses, gloves, or other items.

The construction is fairly straightforward. You only need a few boards and some hardware to get the job done. The joinery is simple to make, including a clever way to allow the front to drop down. And all the joinery can be cut with your table saw and router.

What I like about this drop-front storage center is that it's a small project that you can build in a weekend. Yet, it provides big storage and organization to any entryway. And if the country pine look that you see here is not for you, we've also included a couple of different design options on page 23.

Construction Details

OVERALL DIMENSIONS:
34 1/2" W x 8 3/8" D x 12 1/4" H

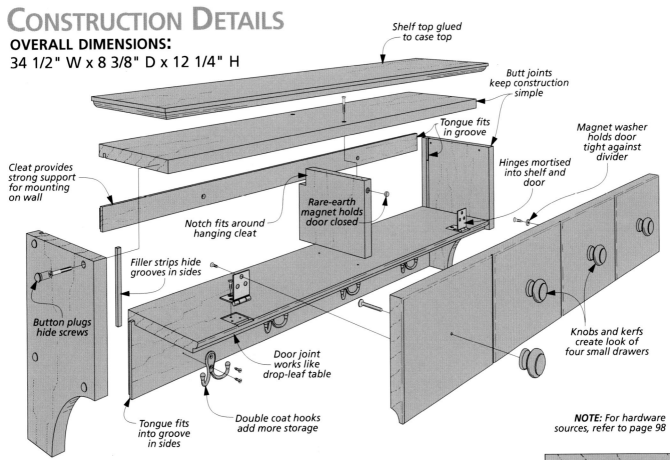

Shelf top glued to case top

Butt joints keep construction simple

Tongue fits in groove

Magnet washer holds door tight against divider

Hinges mortised into shelf and door

Cleat provides strong support for mounting on wall

Rare-earth magnet holds door closed

Notch fits around hanging cleat

Filler strips hide grooves in sides

Button plugs hide screws

Door joint works like drop-leaf table

Knobs and kerfs create look of four small drawers

Tongue fits into groove in sides

Double coat hooks add more storage

NOTE: For hardware sources, refer to page 98

MATERIALS, SUPPLIES & CUTTING DIAGRAM

A	Case Top (1)	$\frac{3}{4}$ x $7\frac{1}{4}$ - $31\frac{1}{2}$
B	Case Bottom (1)	$\frac{3}{4}$ x $7\frac{1}{4}$ - $31\frac{1}{2}$
C	Case Sides (2)	$\frac{3}{4}$ x $7\frac{1}{4}$ - $11\frac{1}{2}$
D	Divider (1)	$\frac{3}{4}$ x $6\frac{3}{4}$ - $5\frac{1}{2}$
E	Back (1)	$\frac{3}{4}$ x $4\frac{3}{4}$ - 32
F	Hanging Cleat (1)	$\frac{3}{4}$ x $1\frac{1}{2}$ - 32
G	Filler Strips (2)	$\frac{1}{4}$ x $\frac{1}{4}$ - $4\frac{3}{4}$
H	Door (1)	$\frac{3}{4}$ x $5\frac{9}{16}$ - $31\frac{3}{8}$
I	Top (1)	$\frac{3}{4}$ x 8 - $34\frac{1}{2}$

- (12) #8 x $1\frac{1}{4}$" Fh Woodscrews
- (1 pr.) $1\frac{1}{4}$" x $1\frac{1}{2}$" Drop-Leaf Hinges w/Screws
- (4) $1\frac{1}{4}$"-dia. Wood Knobs w/Screws
- (10) $\frac{3}{8}$"-dia. Button Plugs
- (1) $\frac{3}{8}$"-dia. Rare-Earth Magnet
- (1) $\frac{3}{8}$"-dia. Magnet Washer
- (1) #6 x $\frac{5}{8}$" Fh Woodscrew
- (4) Brass Double Coat Hooks w/Screws

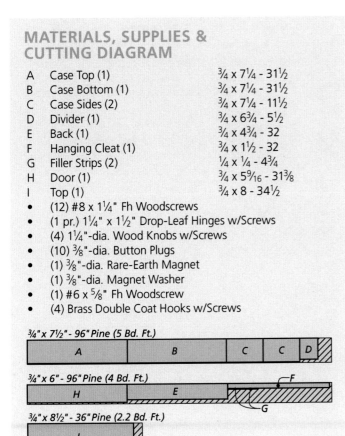

$\frac{3}{4}$"x $7\frac{1}{2}$" - 96" Pine (5 Bd. Ft.)

A	B	C	C	D

$\frac{3}{4}$" x 6" - 96" Pine (4 Bd. Ft.)

H	E	F / G

$\frac{3}{4}$" x $8\frac{1}{2}$" - 36" Pine (2.2 Bd. Ft.)

I

SIDE SECTION VIEW

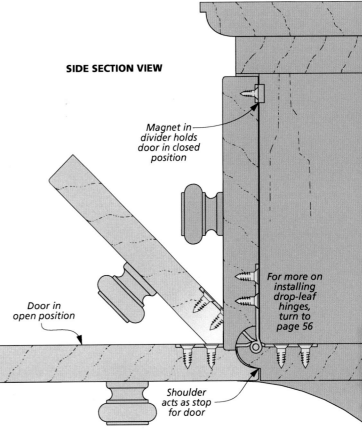

Magnet in divider holds door in closed position

Door in open position

For more on installing drop-leaf hinges, turn to page 56

Shoulder acts as stop for door

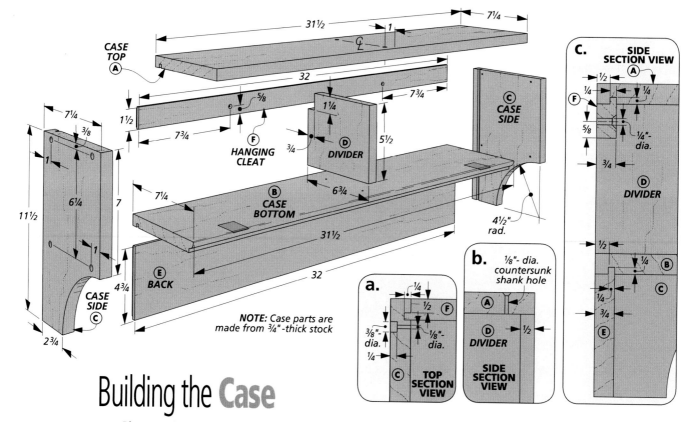

NOTE: Case parts are made from ¾"-thick stock.

Building the Case

If you take a close look at the drawing above, you'll see how the case of the drop-front storage center goes together. It's made up of seven parts: a top and bottom, two sides, a center divider, a cleat

to attach the shelf on a wall, and a back for some hooks.

To keep the project simple, the two side pieces are just screwed to the case top and bottom. But on the inside, there's some tongue and

groove joinery to add stability. And since the sides, top, and bottom of the case have the grooves in them, that's where I started.

TONGUE & GROOVE. The first step is to cut out the top, bottom, and sides. After that, it's over to the table saw to cut the grooves. I start with the grooves because it's easier for me to cut the tongues to fit the grooves than the other way around. The left drawing in the box at left shows how I cut them. These grooves will hold the tongues in the hanging cleat and the back, as you can see details 'a' and 'c' above.

Once that's done, you can set the sides, top, and bottom aside to start working on making the hanging cleat and the back. As I mentioned earlier, you'll need to cut tongues on these parts to fit into the grooves you just made.

The two right drawings in the box at left show how to cut the tongues. But a trick I've learned is to "sneak up" on the fit. Since the grooves are already made, you'll want to purposely cut the tongues a little thick to start. Then, after checking the fit in the grooves, you can raise the blade a bit and trim a

How-To: Tongue & Groove

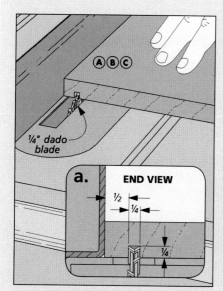

The Groove. Once you have the fence and dado blade set up, you can cut the grooves in the sides, top, and bottom.

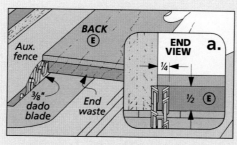
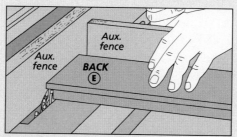

The Tongue. I used a dado blade buried in an auxiliary rip fence to cut the tongues on three sides of the cleat and the back.

little more material off the tongue. Repeat this process until the tongues fit snugly in the grooves.

CURVED PROFILE. With the tongues and grooves cut, you can go ahead and work on the curved profile on the bottom of each case side. Laying out the curve isn't difficult — just draw a 4½"-radius arc on one side. Then, to make sure the curve will match exactly on both side parts, you can temporarily tape the sides together with double-sided tape before making the cut.

Once the curve is laid out, you can cut it out with a band saw, as shown in the Shop Tip at right. When making these types of cuts, I like to stay on the waste side of the layout line and then go back and sand up to the line with a sanding drum. This way, I end up with smooth curves that are the same on both side pieces.

SCREW HOLES. After the curves are sanded smooth, it's time to drill the holes for the screws that will hold the case together (detail 'a,' opposite page). You can also do the same with the case top and bottom,

Shop Tip: Curved Profile

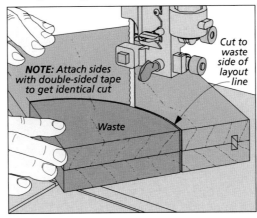

NOTE: Attach sides with double-sided tape to get identical cut

Waste

Cut to waste side of layout line

Cut the Curve on the Band Saw. Be sure to stay on the waste side of the layout line as you cut the curve in the sides of the storage center.

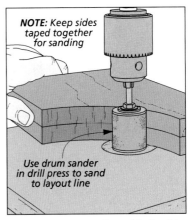

NOTE: Keep sides taped together for sanding

Use drum sander in drill press to sand to layout line

Finish at Drum Sander. With the sides still taped together, use a drum sander to smooth both sides to the layout lines.

which hold the center divider you'll make later (detail 'b'). After the holes are drilled and counterbored, it's a good time to start work on the rule joint for the door.

RULE JOINT. One of the features I like about this project is how the door works. It's similar to a dropleaf table, only upside down.

This is done for more than just looks. A rule joint allows the weight of the door to be distributed evenly along the edge of the case bottom, not just on the hinges. (The Side Section View on page 19 illustrates this.)

The joint combines two matching profiles: a roundover on the case bottom and a cove on the door. When the door is lowered, the cove wraps around the roundover and rests on the shoulder. The box at left shows how to set up to rout the roundover. I'll talk about routing the cove on the door later.

THE DIVIDER. With the case parts complete, you can move on to the divider. After cutting it to size, all you have to do is cut a notch that allows it to fit around the cleat (main drawing on opposite page).

WRAPPING UP. Although the case parts are complete and ready for assembly, I held off putting it together for now. For one thing, it'll be easier to test and adjust the rule joint while everything is apart. And you'll need to align the dropleaf hinges between the door and the case bottom, as you see in the margin photo at right and in the Shop Notebook tip on page 56.

So just set these parts aside for now to start working on the door.

Add the Hinges. Refer to page 56 of Shop Notebook for more information on installing the drop-leaf hinges for the door.

How-To: Bottom Edge Profile

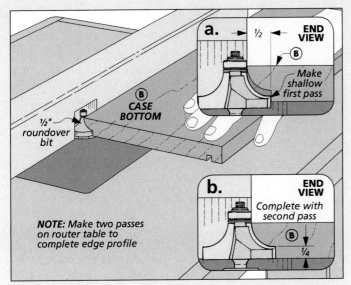

½" roundover bit

CASE BOTTOM

a. ½ END VIEW

B

Make shallow first pass

b. END VIEW

Complete with second pass

B ¼

NOTE: Make two passes on router table to complete edge profile

Rule Joint Profile. To prevent tearout and burning while routing the roundover on the case bottom, start by making a shallow pass. Then you can raise the bit to complete the profile.

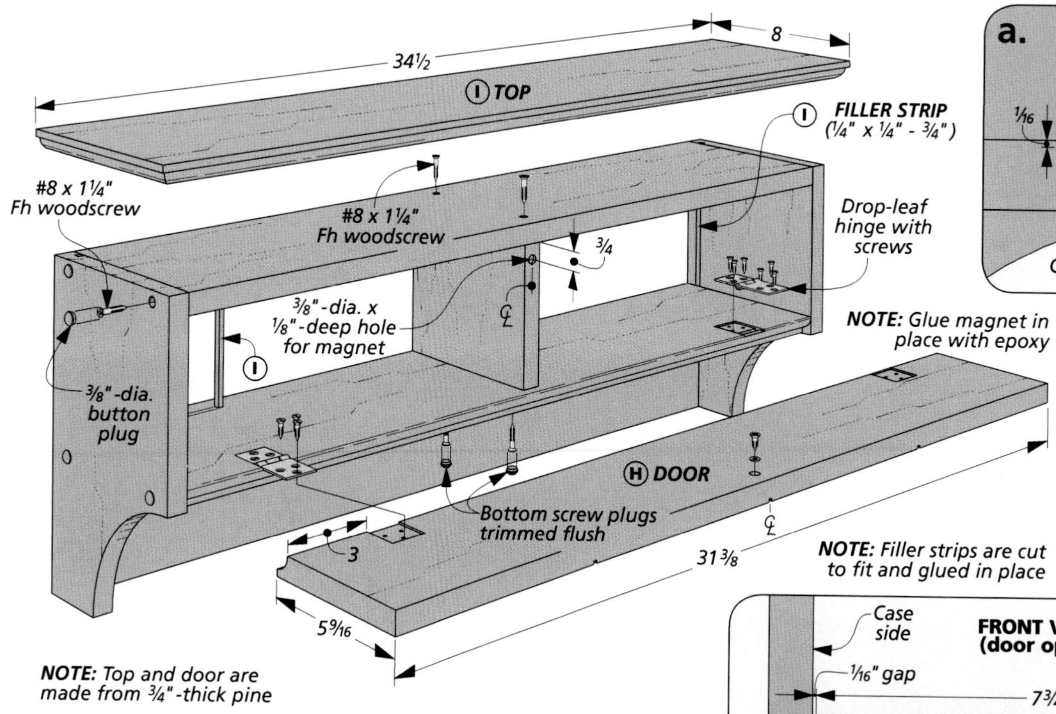
34½
8
Ⓘ TOP
Ⓘ FILLER STRIP
(¼" x ¼" - ¾")
#8 x 1¼"
Fh woodscrew
#8 x 1¼"
Fh woodscrew
Drop-leaf
hinge with
screws
¾
⅜"-dia. x
⅛"-deep hole
for magnet
Ⓘ
⅜"-dia.
button
plug
NOTE: Glue magnet in
place with epoxy
Ⓗ DOOR
Bottom screw plugs
trimmed flush
3
31⅜
5⁹⁄₁₆
NOTE: Filler strips are cut
to fit and glued in place
NOTE: Top and door are
made from ¾"-thick pine

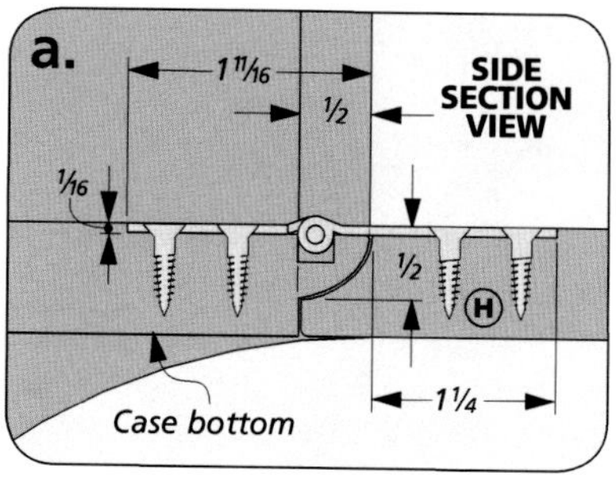
a.
1¹¹⁄₁₆
½
SIDE
SECTION
VIEW
¹⁄₁₆
½
Ⓗ
Case bottom
1¼

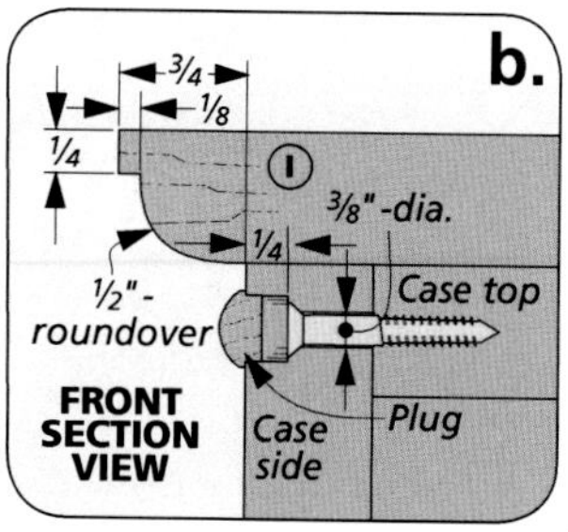
b.
¾
⅛
¼
Ⓘ
⅜"-dia.
¼
Case top
½"-
roundover
FRONT
SECTION
VIEW
Case
side
Plug

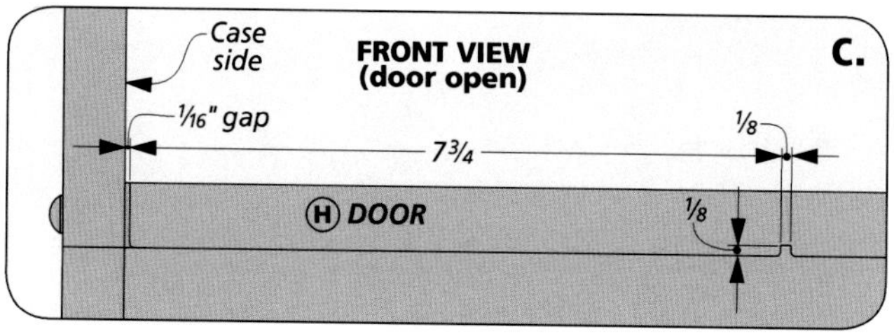
c.
Case
side
FRONT VIEW
(door open)
¹⁄₁₆" gap
7¾
⅛
Ⓗ DOOR
⅛

Completing the Shelf

With the case parts done, it's time to add the final touches. There's a fair amount of work to be done to the door, like completing the rule joint, routing the hinge mortises, and making the "drawers." So that's a good place to start.

DROP-FRONT DOOR. After cutting the door to size, the first step is to rout a cove on its bottom edge (left drawing in the box below). The cove will mate with the round-over on the front edge of the case bottom to create the rule joint.

HINGE MORTISES. The next thing you'll need to do is rout the mortises for the hinges. To make sure the mortises in the door and case bottom were aligned, I laid the door in front of the bottom and marked where they should go, as indicated in the main drawing and detail 'a' above. You can refer to Shop Notebook on page 56 for an explanation of how to mark the locations of the hinges and install them.

MAKE THE "DRAWERS." Once the mortises were cut, I started work on the false drawers. The idea here is to cut equally spaced kerfs in the door to give the appearance that the storage center holds four drawers (detail 'c' above and the right drawing in the box).

Before assembling the case, there are a couple of things left to do. First, drill holes for the knobs (drawing on opposite page). And second, install a magnetic catch (detail 'a' on opposite page). Once these things are completed, you can glue and screw the case together.

SHELF TOP. The next step is to add the top to the case. I routed a ½" roundover with a shoulder along the front edge and the sides (detail 'a,' opposite page). Then, you can simply glue the top to the case.

FILLER STRIPS. There's one final detail before moving on to the finish. Some of the grooves you cut

How-To: Door Shaping

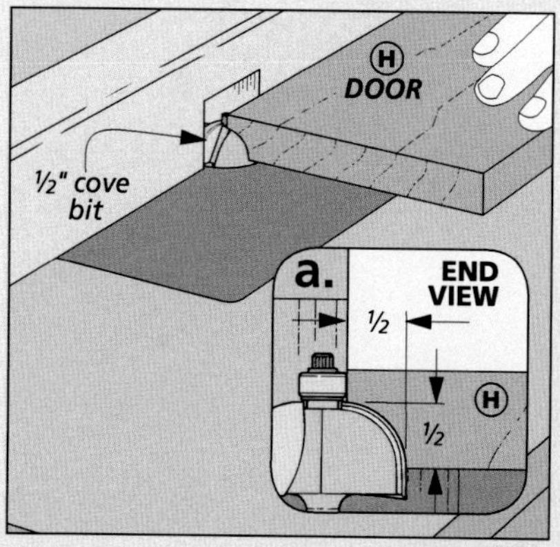
Ⓗ
DOOR
½" cove
bit
a.
END
VIEW
½
Ⓗ
½

The Cove. The profile routed on the bottom edge of the door should mate with the profile of the case bottom.

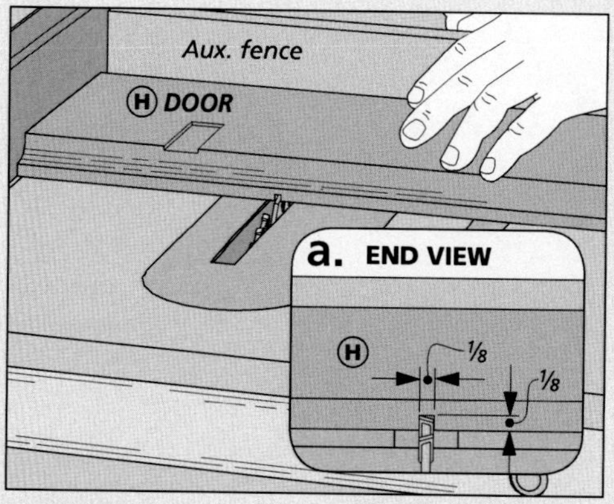
Aux. fence
Ⓗ DOOR
a. END VIEW
Ⓗ
⅛
⅛

Cutting Drawers. Three evenly spaced kerfs cut into the front of the door create the illusion that the storage center contains four small drawers.

earlier are visible on the inside of the case. Although it's not a big deal, I decided to glue in filler strips to give it a more finished look. Now, you're ready to move on to the finishing stage.

FINISHING

To give the shelf an antique look, I decided to "distress" it. That involves taking a couple of tools or a ring full of keys and dropping them randomly on the storage center. But don't get carried away — you want it to look old, not beat up. I also softened some of the edges to add to the worn appearance.

Then, apply a walnut stain to the entire project. When that dries, paint right over the stain. Once the paint dries, lightly sand in different areas to dull it or to allow the stain to peek through. This really adds to the aged look.

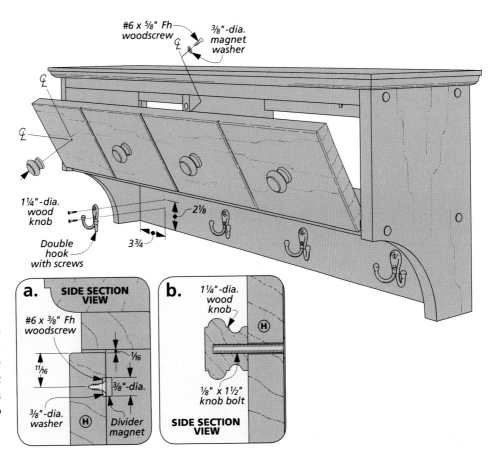

Two Optional **Designs**

While working on the drop-front storage center, I couldn't help but think of a variety of different design options that could easily change the look of this project. A couple of interesting ideas are shown in the drawings here.

For example, you could achieve a more traditional look by changing the edge profile of the top, adding wood pegs, and cutting an ogee profile in the sides. The detail drawings at right can help you with that.

Or, you could go with the straight lines shown in the drawing below for a clean, contemporary look.

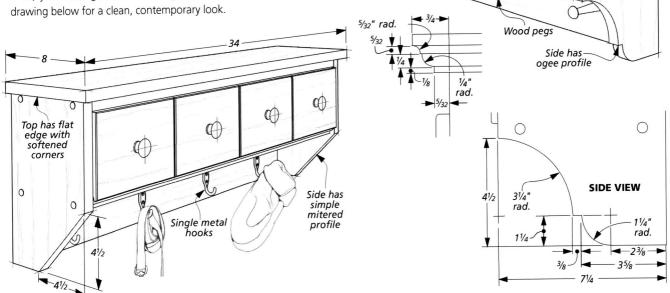

Craftsman-Style
Quilt Rack

With its classic design and interesting details, this accessory is a worthy display for your heirloom treasures.

An heirloom quilt is a work of art and a cherished possession. For this reason alone, it should be on display for everyone to see. And the rack that displays it should reflect a level of craftsmanship that measures up to the skill and time required to make the quilt.

The quilt rack you see above provides the solution. Its Craftsman-style design complements the heirloom quality of the quilt. And it's sturdy enough to display a quilt of any size, plus a few items on top.

Open mortise and tenon joinery provides strength and stability. And keys wedged into square holes at the ends of the stretchers give the project an interesting look. Best of all, you'll be able to cut all the mortises and tenons at your table saw.

CONSTRUCTION DETAILS

OVERALL DIMENSIONS:
32 1/2" W x 11 1/2" D x 32 3/8" H

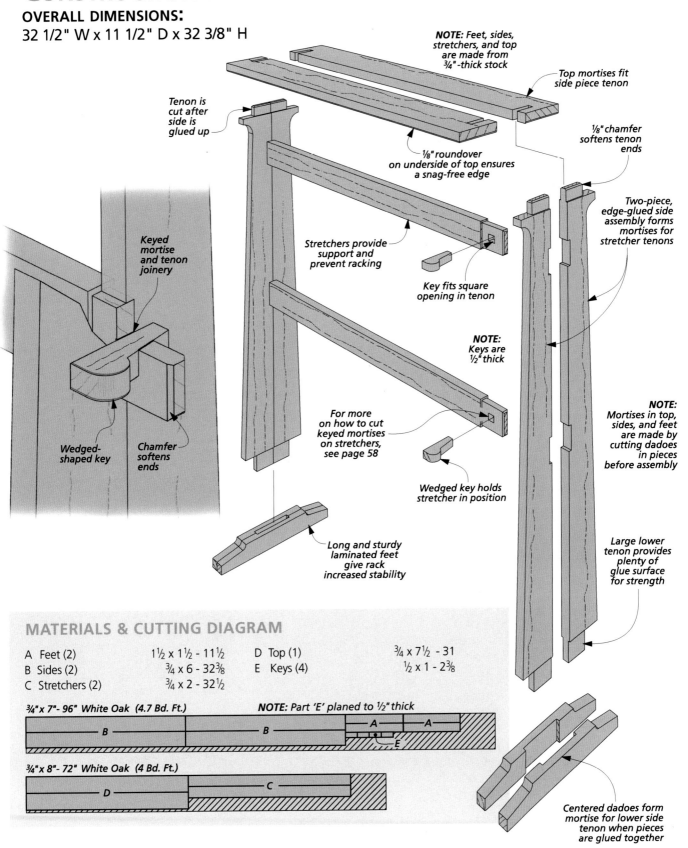

NOTE: Feet, sides, stretchers, and top are made from ¾"-thick stock

Top mortises fit side piece tenon

Tenon is cut after side is glued up

⅛" roundover on underside of top ensures a snag-free edge

⅛" chamfer softens tenon ends

Two-piece, edge-glued side assembly forms mortises for stretcher tenons

Keyed mortise and tenon joinery

Stretchers provide support and prevent racking

Key fits square opening in tenon

NOTE: Keys are ½" thick

Wedged-shaped key

Chamfer softens ends

For more on how to cut keyed mortises on stretchers, see page 58

Wedged key holds stretcher in position

NOTE: Mortises in top, sides, and feet are made by cutting dadoes in pieces before assembly

Large lower tenon provides plenty of glue surface for strength

Long and sturdy laminated feet give rack increased stability

Centered dadoes form mortise for lower side tenon when pieces are glued together

MATERIALS & CUTTING DIAGRAM

A Feet (2)	1½ x 1½ - 11½	
B Sides (2)	¾ x 6 - 32⅜	
C Stretchers (2)	¾ x 2 - 32½	
D Top (1)	¾ x 7½ - 31	
E Keys (4)	½ x 1 - 2⅜	

¾" x 7"- 96" White Oak (4.7 Bd. Ft.)   **NOTE:** Part 'E' planed to ½" thick

B   B   A   A   E

¾"x 8"- 72" White Oak (4 Bd. Ft.)

D   C

Build the Sides & Feet

I began building the quilt rack by making the side assemblies. Each one consists of two parts — a side and a foot. Mortises for connecting the stretchers, top, and feet are made by cutting dadoes in the pieces before assembly.

FOOT. Each foot is made from two pieces of ¾" stock. A dado in each piece forms a mortise for the lower side piece tenon when they're glued together. Begin by setting your dado blade to make a wide cut. Then center a dado through each piece, as shown in the box below.

After cutting the dadoes, I used a spacer block sized to fit the dado, like you see in the photo below, to help keep the parts in alignment during glueup and clamping.

Finally, a trip to the band saw is all it takes to cut the feet to final shape (detail 'c'). Then you're ready to move on to the sides.

BUILD THE SIDES. The sides are made by simply gluing two long pieces of stock together. But before you glue them up, you'll need to cut a couple of mortises to hold the stretchers you'll build later.

You can make the mortises in the sides in the same way you cut the mortises for the feet. Simply turn the workpiece on edge and use

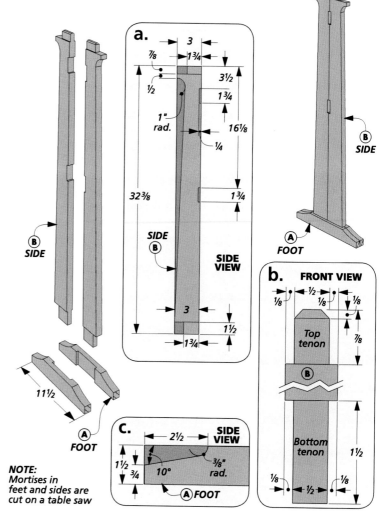

NOTE:
Mortises in feet and sides are cut on a table saw

your dado blade to cut notches on each of the side pieces.

END TENONS. Now glue up the sides, and cut a tenon at each end (details 'a' and 'b' and the box on page 27).

Finally, cut the sides to rough shape. Then all that's left is to make a template and use a flush-trim bit to trim each side to final size (lower right photo on the next page).

How-To: Mortises on a Table Saw

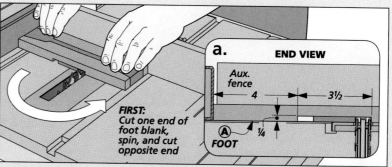

Spacer Block for Alignment. A spacer block sized to fit each mortise maintains alignment of the mortises when the pieces are glued and clamped together.

Centered Mortise. Use a wide dado blade to cut the foot mortise. Just set the depth of the cut and position the rip fence to make the first pass. Then flip the blank, make a second pass, and remove the waste in between.

Complete the Rack

With the sides completed, you're now ready to build the stretchers. The stretchers are one of the most interesting parts of the quilt rack. A tenon on each end has a square opening to accept a hardwood key. The key locks the stretcher in the mortise to hold the rack together.

MAKE THE STRETCHERS. After cutting the stretchers to size, cut tenons on each end, as shown in details 'a' and 'd.' Again, I used a wide dado blade setup. Just set the saw blade to depth and cut the shoulders and cheeks. To soften the ends of the tenons, I chamfered the edges.

Next, square an opening in the tenon to accept a key (detail 'a'). You'll also need to make keys to wedge into the tenons (detail 'c'). It's a good idea to take a little time here to make sure the hole is tapered to match the key. Turn to page 58 to learn more about making these tenons and the keys.

THE TOP. The last thing left to do is add a top to the rack. It has mortises similar to those on the sides to accept the upper side tenons.

You can make the top in much the same way you built the sides. You'll need to locate a notch in each top piece (drawing and detail 'b' above). I used the same technique

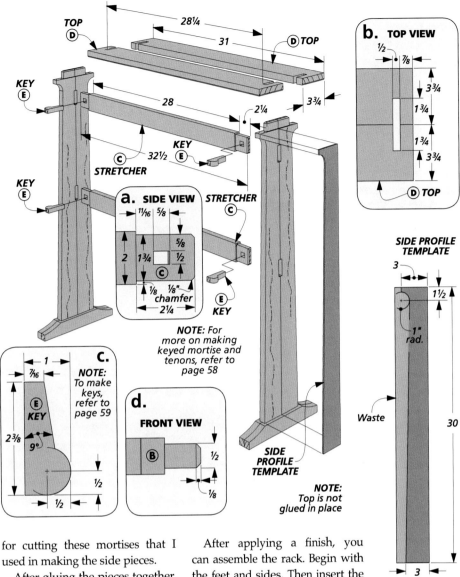

for cutting these mortises that I used in making the side pieces.

After gluing the pieces together, I routed an 1/8" roundover along the bottom for a snag-free edge.

After applying a finish, you can assemble the rack. Begin with the feet and sides. Then insert the stretchers and keys, add the top, and it's ready to display a quilt.

Tenons on a Table Saw

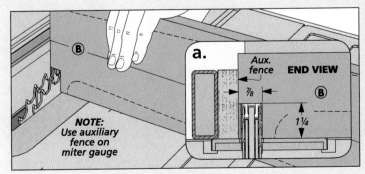

Side Tenons. After setting the dado blade to the correct height, turn the workpiece on edge. Then use the miter gauge and an auxiliary fence to keep the workpiece aligned for the cut.

Perfectly Shaped Sides. After the side piece is cut to rough size, you can use a template and your router with a flush-trim bit to trim the piece to a smooth final shape.

Paneled Window Seat

Some basic materials and simple joinery add up to a great-looking project.

Design Option. This beadboard paneled storage chest starts with the same "framed" plywood box. I just changed a few of the details for a less formal look.

You'll probably run into just one problem when you build this window seat — convincing your friends that it only took a couple of days to build. It looks much too nice to be so easy.

You start by building a simple plywood box. A sheet of plywood and a little bit of basic joinery is all it takes. Next, you cover this "shell" with solid-wood framing and add some traditional molding. Glue, brads, and a handful of screws hold it all together. In no time, the basic plywood box is transformed into a classic.

One of the shortcuts that makes this possible is using pre-made moldings purchased at a home center. This saves a lot of work with no sacrifice in quality.

And if the casual look of the beadboard paneled chest shown at left grabs you, it's an easy change. Get that look by adding different details to the same box and frame.

A Plywood Box

The drawing at right shows how to get started by putting together a sturdy plywood box. To keep weight down, I used ½" plywood.

THE JOINERY. The box needs to be solidly built but also easy to assemble. So I used some basic joinery that serves both purposes. As you see in detail 'a,' the ends of the box sides are rabbeted to hold the ends. This gives you plenty of glue surface and allows you to easily line up the corners during assembly.

The bottom is firmly captured in grooves cut into the inside faces of all four panels (detail 'b'). So it will stay put under the heaviest loads. And woodscrews take the place of clamps during the glue-up.

THE RABBETS. Once the box sides and box ends are cut to size, the next step is to cut rabbets in the sides. For this, I installed a dado blade on the table saw and "buried" it in an auxiliary fence (box below).

The width of these rabbets should match the thickness of the plywood you're using. (The plywood is often a bit undersized.) And a consistent depth is just as important. A simple hold-down will keep the plywood panels flat on the table saw for an easier and more accurate cut (photo below).

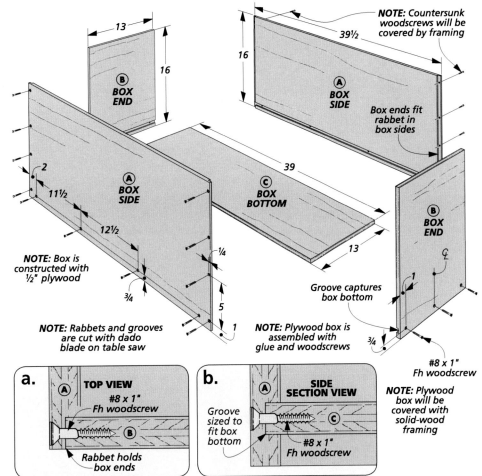

NOTE: Countersunk woodscrews will be covered by framing

Box ends fit rabbet in box sides

Groove captures box bottom

#8 x 1" Fh woodscrew

NOTE: Plywood box will be covered with solid-wood framing

NOTE: Box is constructed with ½" plywood

NOTE: Rabbets and grooves are cut with dado blade on table saw

NOTE: Plywood box is assembled with glue and woodscrews

a. TOP VIEW
#8 x 1" Fh woodscrew
Rabbet holds box ends

b. SIDE SECTION VIEW
Groove sized to fit box bottom
#8 x 1" Fh woodscrew

THE GROOVES. After cutting the rabbets, switch to a narrower dado blade to cut the grooves that capture the bottom panel. Just like the rabbets in the side panels, you want a snug fit. So as shown below, this is a "two pass" operation. The first cut does most of the work. And after adjusting the fence, a second cut completes the job.

MAKE A BOX. With the bottom cut to size, assemble the box with countersunk woodscrews and glue. Then start adding the "extras."

How-To: Cutting Rabbets & Grooves

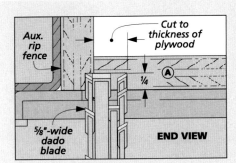

Aux. rip fence — Cut to thickness of plywood — ⅝"-wide dado blade — END VIEW

Rabbets. Cutting the rabbets in the ends of the side panels is a job for a dado blade buried in an auxiliary rip fence. Just match the width of the rabbet to the thickness of the plywood.

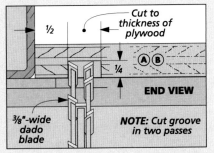

Cut to thickness of plywood — ½ — ⅜"-wide dado blade — NOTE: Cut groove in two passes — END VIEW

Grooves. A narrower dado blade is used to cut tight-fitting grooves in the sides and ends of the box to hold the bottom. The second of two passes sizes the groove accurately.

Shop Tip

Hold-Down. A simple shop-made hold-down makes the job of cutting the rabbets and the grooves in the plywood panels a little easier.

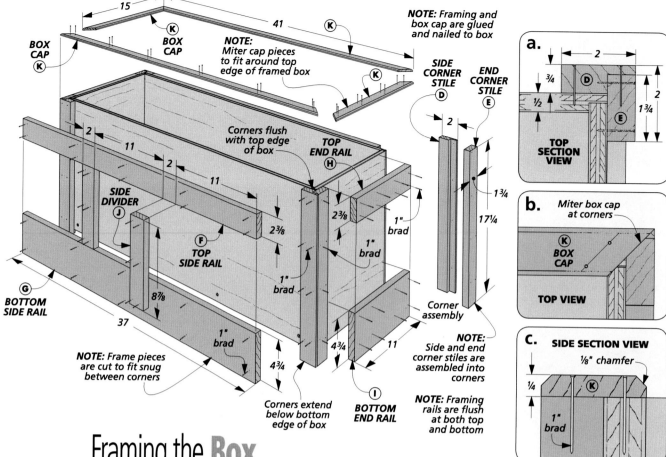

Framing the Box

Once the box is assembled, the next step is to add the solid-wood frame shown in the drawing above. Since all the frame parts are nailed and glued to the plywood box, I kept the joinery to a minimum.

THE CORNERS. The first job is to make and install the four preassembled corners. A glance at detail 'a' shows how they go together. Just like the plywood box, a rabbeted corner joint adds strength and eases the assembly. The "pocket" created by the rabbet in the side stiles firmly captures the end stile. This gives you a strong flush corner that's easy to install.

Start by cutting the side corner stiles and the narrower end corner stiles to size from ¾"-thick stock. When the narrower end stiles are fit into the rabbet in the side stiles, the result is an equal "reveal" on the corners (detail 'a').

Once the stiles are cut to size, the next task is to use the dado blade to rabbet the side stiles. Just match the width of the rabbet to the thickness of the end stiles for a flush fit.

When you're through at the table saw, the stiles can be assembled (glue and brads) into corners. And finally, the corners are glued and nailed in place on the box, flush to the top edge (detail 'a').

THE FRAME. Completing the framing goes quickly. First, cut the top and bottom side rails and end rails to width and rough length. Then cut each rail to fit snug in between the corners. Use glue and brads to fasten them in place. Finally, you can cut the side dividers to fit and add them to the frame.

A CAP. To complete the framing, I applied a cap to the top edge of the box. This piece hides the plywood edge and the joint between the framing and the box. Cut the box cap to size and chamfer both edges before mitering it to fit, as you see in details 'b' and 'c.'

Shop Tip: Setting the Brads

The only drawback to using brads is that you have to hide them. But this is simply a matter of "setting" them.

When I do this, I try to avoid getting "hammer dings" by leaving the nails slightly proud of the wood surface. Then a fine-point nail set takes over to drive the nail far enough below the surface so that it can be completely hidden with a little bit of wood putty (about ¹⁄₁₆").

Trimming It Out

With the framing on the box completed, you can begin to add a little window dressing. I wanted to give the box a more formal look with a wrapped base and some "panel" molding. But I didn't want to make a lot of extra work. The answer was to use stock moldings purchased from a local home improvement store. These "fancy" moldings would have been much too difficult and time consuming to make, and the cost was pretty reasonable.

TRIMMING THE BASE. I thought the base of the box needed a solid foundation with a little extra detail. For this job, I picked out some colonial-style base molding. The base that I found was about 5" wide, which was a little out of proportion to the scale of the box. So before fitting it to the box, I took it to the table saw and ripped it to 3¾" in width (detail 'a'). This size still had the solid feel I wanted but fit the box better.

Once the base molding is cut to width, it's just a matter of mitering it to fit the box. Use the miter-to-fit technique that you used for the cap molding. As each piece is cut, glue and nail it in place flush to the bottom edge of the corners (detail 'b'). Work around the box until you end up back where you started.

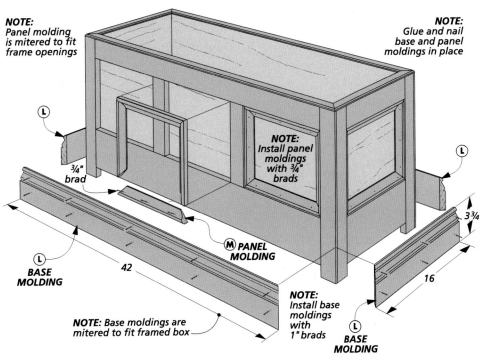

NOTE: Panel molding is mitered to fit frame openings

NOTE: Glue and nail base and panel moldings in place

NOTE: Install panel moldings with ¾" brads

L

¾" brad

L

3¾

L
BASE MOLDING

42

M PANEL MOLDING

NOTE: Install base moldings with 1" brads

16

BASE MOLDING

NOTE: Base moldings are mitered to fit framed box

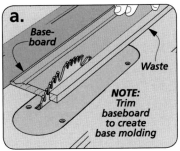

a.

Baseboard

Waste

NOTE: Trim baseboard to create base molding

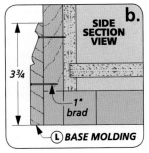

b.

SIDE SECTION VIEW

3¾

1" brad

L BASE MOLDING

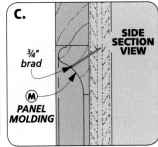

c.

SIDE SECTION VIEW

¾" brad

M PANEL MOLDING

PANEL MOLDING. The panel molding (sold as cap molding) that I bought to install around the inside of the framed panels was a perfect complement to the colonial base. You'll need enough to frame all of the "panels," and the procedure is simple. As you did for the base molding, miter one piece to fit and glue and nail it in place (detail 'c'). Then work around the openings to fit the remaining pieces.

How-To: Miter Moldings to Perfection

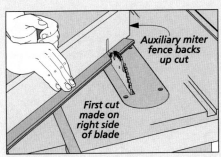

Auxiliary miter fence backs up cut

First cut made on right side of blade

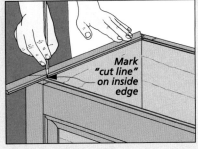

Mark "cut line" on inside edge

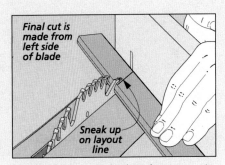

Final cut is made from left side of blade

Sneak up on layout line

Miter One End. Using this miter-to-fit technique, you don't need to rely on "hard" measurements. Simply start by mitering one end of an extra-long workpiece.

Make Your Mark. Next, set the mitered piece in place to mark for the second cut. A pencil line on the inside edge of the workpiece will show you where to cut.

The Final Cut. Now, back at the saw, you're ready for the second cut. Working from the left side of the blade, you can sneak up on your mark for a perfect fit.

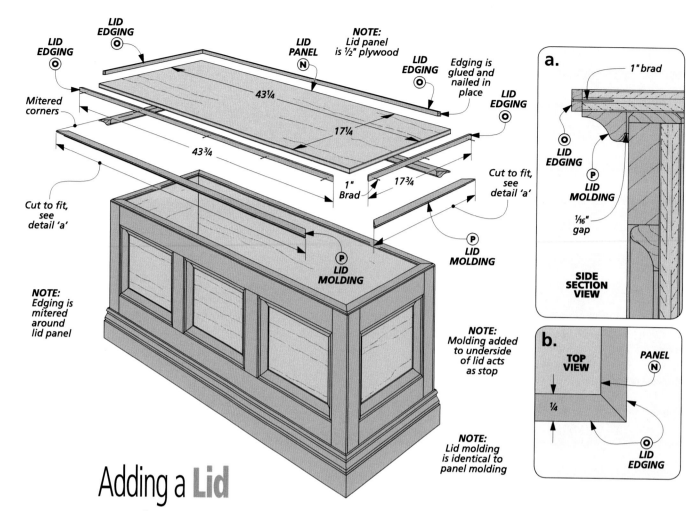

LID EDGING

LID EDGING

LID EDGING

LID PANEL Ⓝ

NOTE: Lid panel is ½" plywood

LID EDGING

LID EDGING

Edging is glued and nailed in place

Mitered corners

43¼

17¼

Cut to fit, see detail 'a'

Cut to fit, see detail 'a'

43¾

1" Brad

17¾

NOTE: Edging is mitered around lid panel

Ⓟ

Ⓟ **LID MOLDING**

Ⓟ **LID MOLDING**

NOTE: Molding added to underside of lid acts as stop

NOTE: Lid molding is identical to panel molding

a.

1" brad

Ⓞ **LID EDGING**

Ⓟ **LID MOLDING**

1/16" gap

SIDE SECTION VIEW

b.

TOP VIEW

PANEL Ⓝ

¼

Ⓞ **LID EDGING**

Adding a Lid

At this point, the box looks pretty sharp. But for a window seat, it lacks one important part: a solid lid or seat to cover the box. And again, I took the easy route. Rather than make a tricky-to-install, hinged lid, I went with a simple, lift-off lid.

HOW IT FITS. In the drawing above, you'll see how this lid is put together. With no hinges to hold it in place, I needed a different way to keep the lid on the box. I did this by using the same molding used to frame the panels as a "lid stop."

Added to the underside of the lid panel, it keeps the lid in place and also adds depth and detail.

BUILD IT. The same ½" plywood used for the box will do nicely for the lid. Start by cutting the lid panel to size. Next, to hide the edges of the plywood, make enough edging to wrap the lid panel (I used leftover framing scraps). Apply it as you did the previous mitered pieces (details 'a' and 'b').

LID MOLDING. After the edging is in place and sanded flush, the lid molding can be added to the bottom of the lid. The box at left shows the process. Working with the box and lid upside down makes the job of fitting the molding a lot easier.

You want the lid to fit tightly but still be easy to lift on and off. So I used spacers to create a 1/16" clearance on all sides.

Once the lid molding has been installed, all you need to do is fill the brad holes, do a little sanding, and you're ready to paint.

How-To: Get the Right Fit

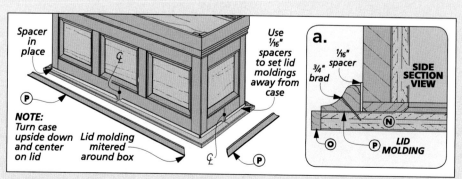

Spacer in place

Use 1/16" spacers to set lid moldings away from case

a.

1/16" spacer

¾" brad

SIDE SECTION VIEW

Ⓟ

Ⓝ

Ⓞ

Ⓟ **LID MOLDING**

NOTE: Turn case upside down and center on lid

Lid molding mitered around box

Ⓟ

Turn It Upside Down. It's much easier to accurately fit the cap molding to the lid if you turn the whole works upside down. With the box centered on the lid and some spacers in place, simply miter the lid molding to fit and install it just as you have the other moldings.

A Different Look: Beadboard

The "casual" beadboard chest shown in the drawing at right and in the lower left photo on page 28 has the same basic structure as its more formal cousin. But a few simple changes give it a very different appearance.

First, I traded the wrapped base for a simple chamfer on the bottom of the "legs." And the frame openings are covered with beadboard. I topped the chest with a naturally finished pine lid loosely held in position by cleats. This version is just as easy to build and looks just as nice.

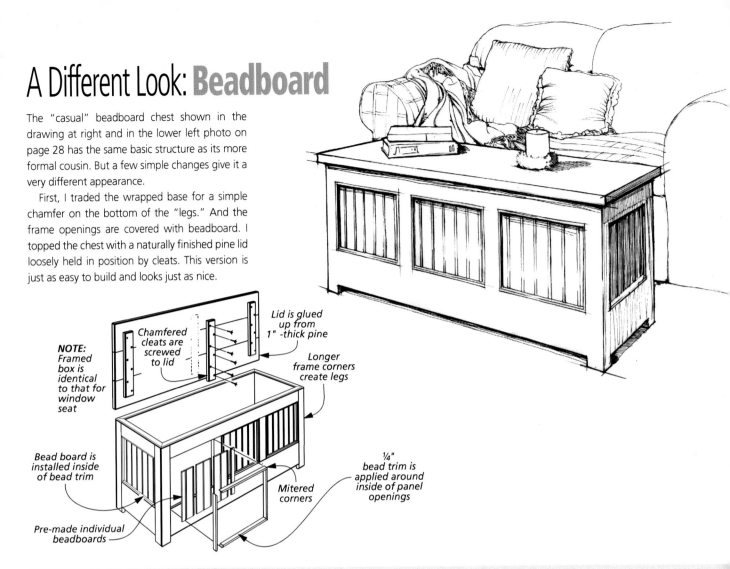

Lid is glued up from 1"-thick pine

Chamfered cleats are screwed to lid

Longer frame corners create legs

NOTE: Framed box is identical to that for window seat

Bead board is installed inside of bead trim

¼" bead trim is applied around inside of panel openings

Mitered corners

Pre-made individual beadboards

MATERIALS, SUPPLIES & CUTTING DIAGRAM

A	Box Sides (2)	½ ply. - 16 x 39½
B	Box Ends (2)	½ ply. - 16 x 13
C	Box Bottom (1)	½ ply. - 13 x 39
D	Side Corner Stiles (4)	¾ x 2 - 17¼
E	End Corner Stiles (4)	¾ x 1¾ - 17¼
F	Top Side Rails (2)	¾ x 2⅜ - 37
G	Bottom Side Rails (2)	¾ x 4¾ - 37
H	Top End Rails (2)	¾ x 2⅜ - 11
I	Bottom End Rails (2)	¾ x 4¾ - 11
J	Side Dividers (4)	¾ x 2 - 8⅞
K	Box Cap (1)	¼ x 1¼ - 120 rgh.
L	Base Molding (1)	⁹⁄₁₆ x 3¾ - 144 rgh.

M	Panel Molding (3)	⅝ x 1⅛ - 120 rgh.
N	Lid Panel (1)	½ ply. - 17¼ x 43¼
O	Lid Edging (1)	¼ x ½ - 130 rgh.
P	Lid Molding (1)	⅝ x 1⅛ - 144 rgh.

- (4) Bun Feet
- (248) 1" Brads
- (112) ¾" Brads

ALSO NEEDED: 12' of Colonial base molding for part L; 22' of cap molding for parts M and P; and a sheet of ½"-thick Birch plywood for parts A, B, and C

¾" x 9" - 96" Poplar (6 Bd. Ft.)

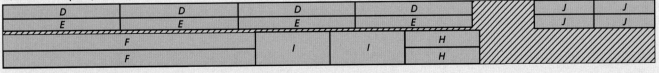

¾" x 9" - 96" Poplar (6 Bd. Ft.)

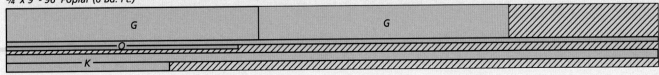

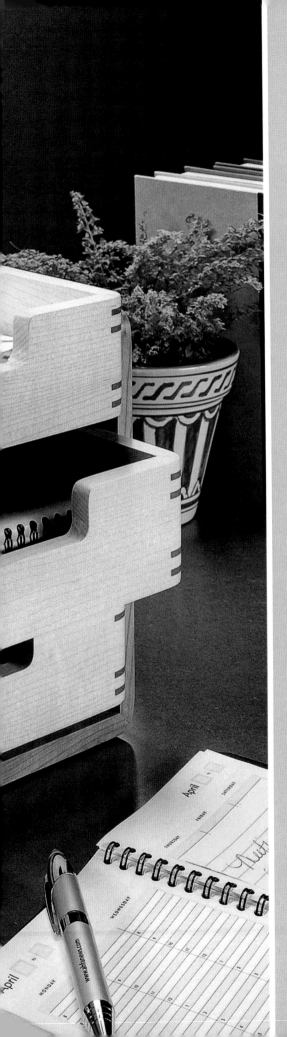

Home
Office

Organize your desktop with any of these attractive, hand-crafted projects. Each one features simple details plus compartments to keep papers and supplies close at hand.

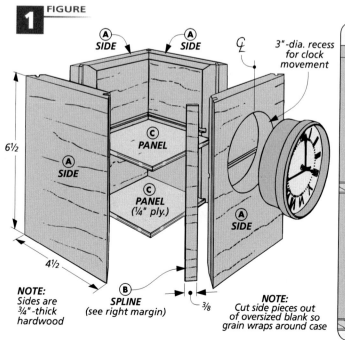

Desk Clock

This may look like an ordinary desk clock, but there's more to it than meets the eye.

More techniques are used in building this clock than you'd expect — miter and spline joints, veneering, and template routing to name a few. To add one more element, the top lifts off to reveal a secret compartment. All this, and you'll still complete it in a weekend.

CASE

The case of the clock is made of four identical sides joined with miters and splines. It also has two bottoms. One sits flush with the bottom of the case. The other bottom is positioned halfway up to form a shallow compartment under the top.

SIDES. To build the clock, I started with the sides. As you can see in the photo, the grain runs horizontally. I did this for two reasons. First, I wanted the grain to wrap around the case. More importantly, as the wood expands and contracts across the grain, the miter joints of the base molding won't open up.

To make the sides, begin by ripping an extra-long piece of ¾" stock to final width. Working with an extra-long piece is safer and means fewer passes over the table saw. Before mitering the blank to length, the first thing I did was cut a chamfer along one edge of the blank, as Figure 2 shows. This simply relieves the sharp, top edge of the compartment (Figure 1).

With the chamfer cut, the next step is to cut a groove for the panel (Figure 3). You'll need to sneak up on the depth of the groove so the plywood panel will fit snug. The last thing to do on the oversized blank is to cut a rabbet sized to hold a ¼" plywood bottom (Figure 3b). Again, you'll want to do this in a few passes so the plywood sits flush with the bottom of the case.

MITER CUT. Now the sides can be cut from the blank. This will be a two-step process. And the important thing is that you try to allow as little waste between the pieces as possible. This way, the grain will look like it wraps around the case.

1 FIGURE

- (A) SIDE
- (A) SIDE
- C̸L
- 3"-dia. recess for clock movement
- (C) PANEL
- (A) SIDE
- (C) PANEL (¼" ply.)
- (A) SIDE
- 6½
- 4½
- (B) SPLINE (see right margin)
- ⅜

NOTE: Sides are ¾"-thick hardwood

NOTE: Cut side pieces out of oversized blank so grain wraps around case

a.

- ¼
- (A)
- (A)
- SIDE SECTION VIEW
- 2½
- 3"-dia. recess for clock
- (C)
- ⅝
- (C)

The first step is to miter the pieces to rough length. (I cut mine 4⅝" long.) Here, the blade should tilt away from the fence so the workpiece isn't trapped under the blade. Then, reposition the rip fence and cut the sides to final length (4½").

SPLINES. To strengthen the miters, I decided to add splines. Cutting the kerfs for the splines is easy. Since the blade is already set to 45°, all you need to do is reposition the fence (Figure 4). Then to cut the splines safely, I used a two-pass method, as indicated in the margin. The first thing to do is cut some kerfs in both edges of an oversized blank. Then lay the blank on its face, and cut the splines to width.

CLOCK HOLE. With the sides nearly finished, choose one of the sides so you can cut the recess for the clock movement. As you can see in the lower margin photo, you could use a saw-tooth Forstner bit to do this, but I used a router with a guide bushing and a hardboard template. For more information on making the template, turn to page 55.

With the template in hand, it can be attached to the workpiece with double-sided tape. Because the hole is ⅝" deep, you'll want to rout out the waste in a few passes (Figure 5a). As you make the last pass, don't be worried if you see the groove for the bottom. This won't affect the fit of the bottom or the clock movement.

After cutting two ¼" plywood panels to fit the groove and rabbet, the case is ready to be assembled.

ASSEMBLY. It takes a little work to get all the workpieces put together and the corners square. So I decided to use *Franklin's Titebond Extend Wood Glue* to give me extra time.

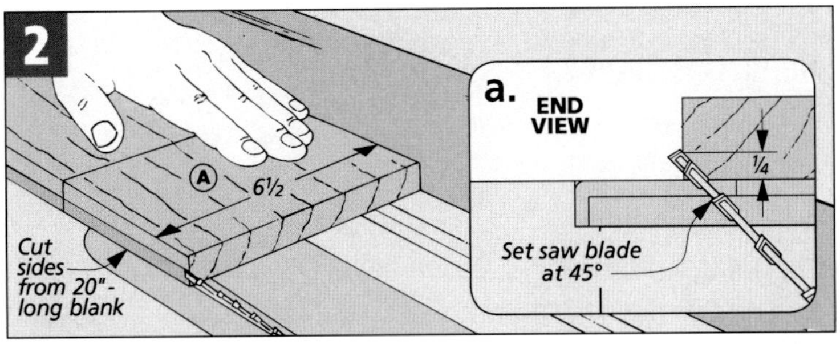
2
A
6½
Cut sides from 20"-long blank
a. END VIEW
¼
Set saw blade at 45°

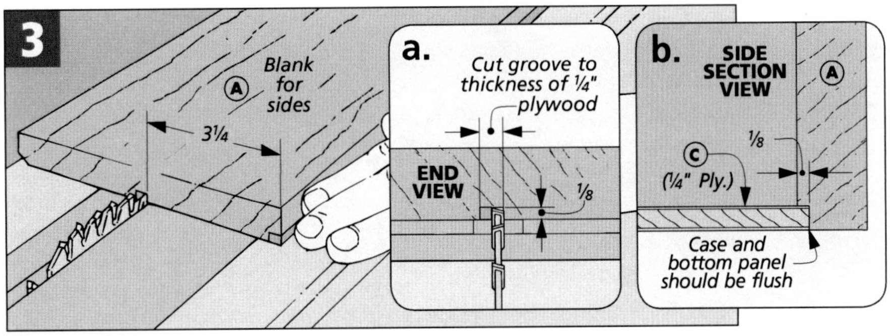
3
Blank for sides
A
3¼
a.
Cut groove to thickness of ¼" plywood
END VIEW
⅛
b. SIDE SECTION VIEW
A
C
(¼" Ply.)
⅛
Case and bottom panel should be flush

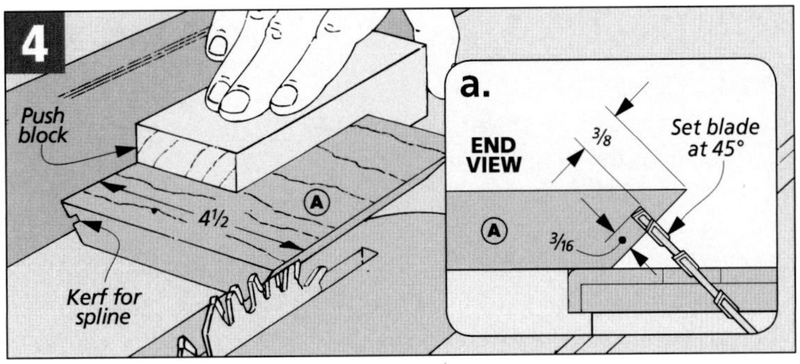
4
Push block
4½
A
Kerf for spline
a.
END VIEW
⅜
Set blade at 45°
A
3/16

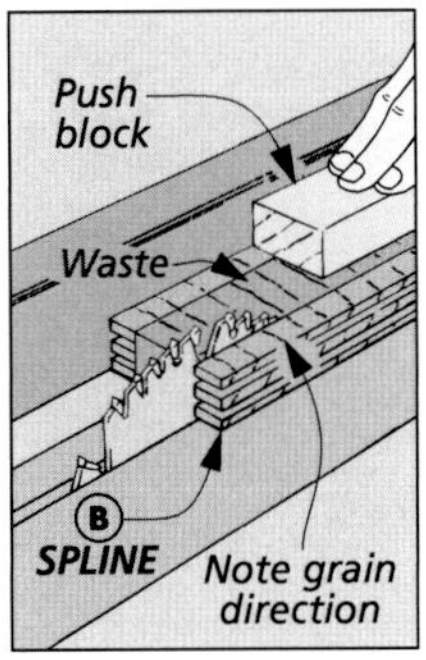
Push block
Waste
B
SPLINE
Note grain direction

Splines for Miters. Cut kerfs on the edges of an oversized blank. Then, lay the blank face down, and cut the splines free.

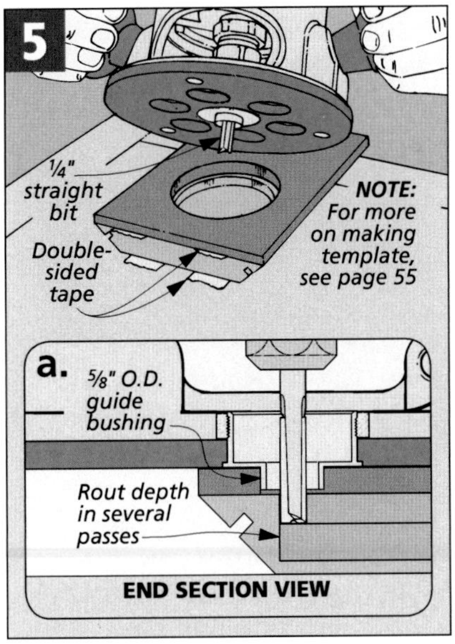
5
¼" straight bit
Double-sided tape
NOTE: For more on making template, see page 55
a.
⅝" O.D. guide bushing
Rout depth in several passes
END SECTION VIEW

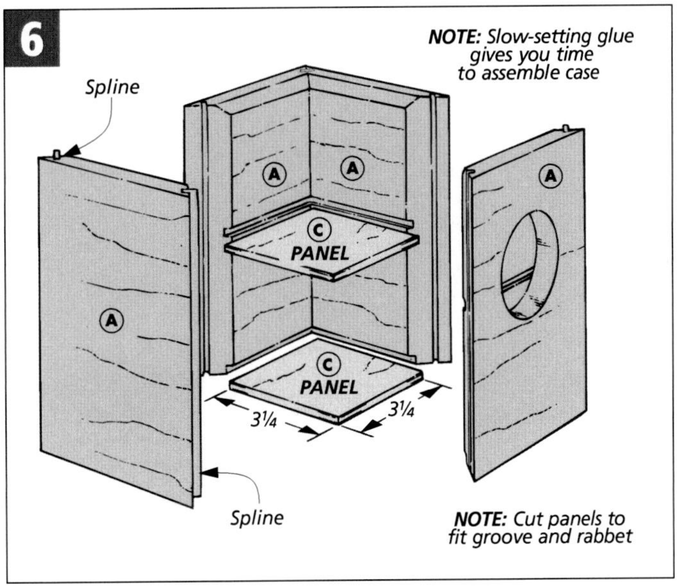
6
Spline
NOTE: Slow-setting glue gives you time to assemble case
A
A
A
C
PANEL
A
C
PANEL
3¼
3¼
Spline
NOTE: Cut panels to fit groove and rabbet

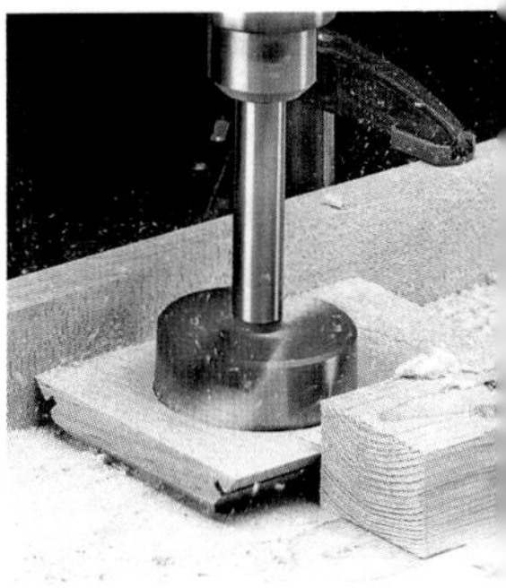

Create a Recess. A Forstner bit makes quick work of drilling the hole for the clock movement. For another option, turn to page 55 of Shop Notebook.

Building the Lid

The case isn't quite complete yet, but for now, you'll need to set it aside and work on the removable lid. If you take a close look at the photo at left, you can see the reason why. The lid fits over a rabbet that's cut in the top of the case. And by building the lid first, it's a lot easier to sneak up on the size of the rabbet to end up with a perfect fit.

I built the lid out of a laminated panel and two layers of molding. And for contrast, I made the lower molding out of cherry.

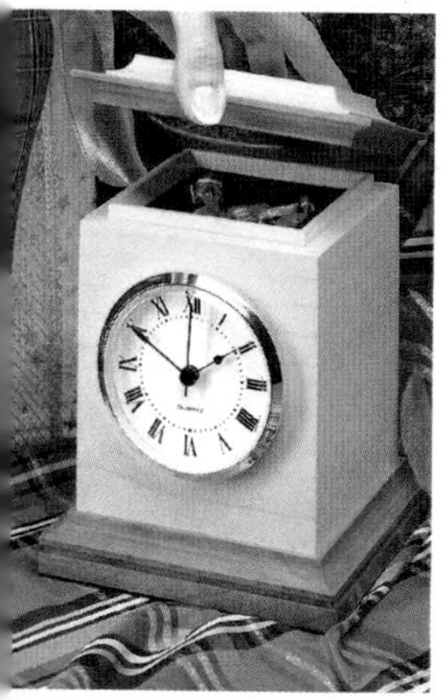

Inside the Clock. The lid of the clock lifts off to reveal a felt-lined compartment that's great for storing small items.

LID PANEL. I started by making the panel assembly because all the other parts will wrap around it. This assembly starts as a sandwich of two plywood panels, good faces out, and a veneer of bird's eye maple (Figure 7).

The next step is to create a tongue around the panel assembly that the upper molding will be glued to. To do this, you need to cut a rabbet on each edge. Figure 7a shows how I cut the rabbets on the router table using a straight bit and fence.

MOLDING. With the lid panel finished, you can begin on the molding pieces. As you see in Figure 8, these pieces are pretty small. If you tried to shape them individually, there wouldn't be much to hold on to. To get around this, each layer of molding is mitered and glued to the lid panel first. The larger square formed by the molding and lid creates a safe workpiece to handle on the router table (Figure 9).

For the upper molding, I cut a groove in an extra-long piece of maple on the table saw. The goal is for the molding to end up flush with the lid panel, so you'll have to make several passes, testing for fit after each pass (Figure 8a).

Now you're ready to miter the upper molding to fit around the lid panel and glue it in place.

With the upper layer in place, you can begin creating the profile. There are two steps to this. First, I cut a shallow rabbet in the bottom of the molding (Figure 9a). This rabbet simply helps you position the lower molding that's added later. Second, rout a cove around the top of the molding (Figure 9b).

The second layer of molding is similar to the first. But it's even easier to make. Like the first, the lower molding starts off as a ¾"-thick blank that's mitered and

FIGURE 7

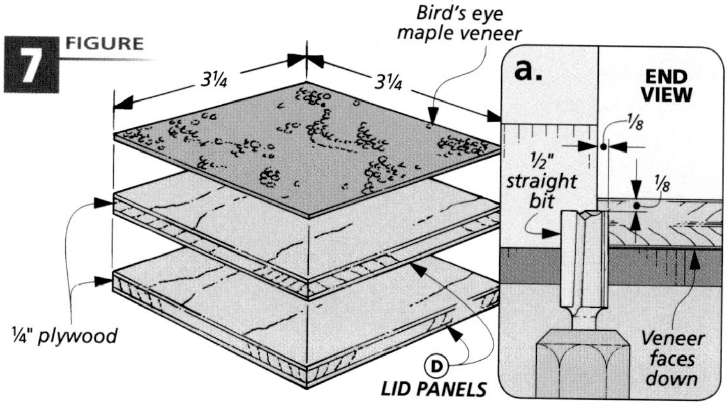

Bird's eye maple veneer
3¼
3¼
¼" plywood
D
LID PANELS
a.
END VIEW
1/8
½" straight bit
1/8
Veneer faces down

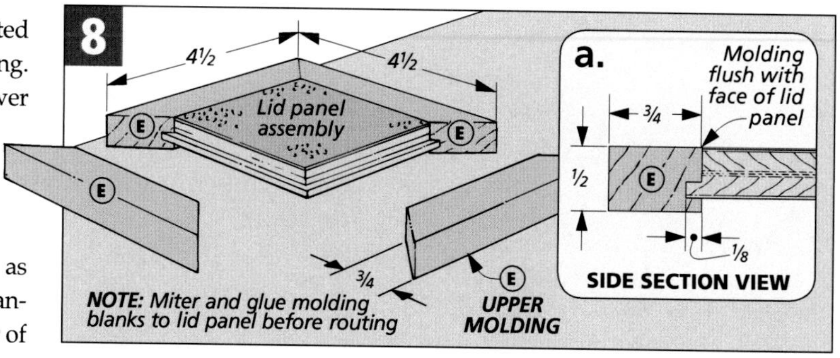

8
4½
4½
Lid panel assembly
E
E
E
E
¾
NOTE: Miter and glue molding blanks to lid panel before routing
UPPER MOLDING
a.
Molding flush with face of lid panel
¾
½
1/8
SIDE SECTION VIEW

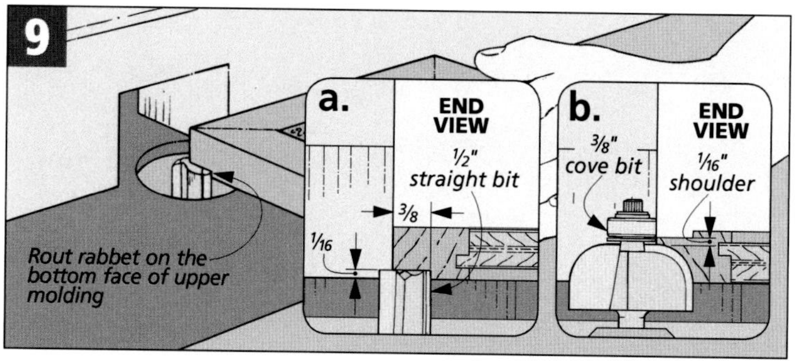

9
Rout rabbet on the bottom face of upper molding
a.
END VIEW
½" straight bit
3/8
1/16
b.
END VIEW
3/8" cove bit
1/16" shoulder

FIGURE 10

W4422A10

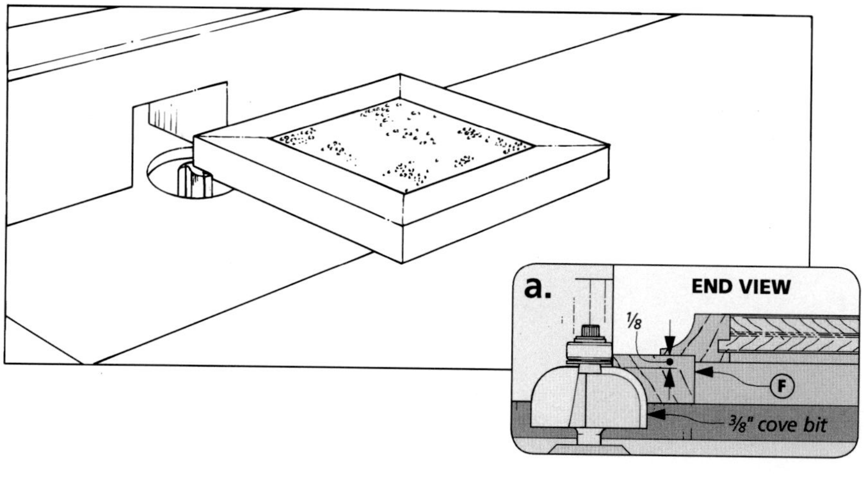

a.
END VIEW
1/8
F
3/8" cove bit

glued around the lid, as you can see in Figure 10. The final step in making the lid is to rout a cove in the bottom (Figure 10a).

RABBET CASE. Although the lid is finished, it won't fit on the case — you still need to cut a rabbet on the case. By waiting until now to cut the rabbet, I was able to easily get a snug fit with the lid.

To cut the rabbet, I decided to use a straight bit in the router table (Figures 11 and 11a). This way I could get smooth shoulders. I nibbled away until the lid just slipped over the rabbet (Figure 11b).

BASE MOLDING. Now that the rabbet has been cut in the top of the case, you can finish up by adding the contrasting molding to the bottom (Figure 12). Because the final size of the pieces is small, it's safer to form them on an oversized blank.

There are only three steps to the base molding. First, cut a kerf for a shadow line on the blank (Figure 12a). Second, rout a cove on the router table leaving a slight shoulder between the cove and the shadow line you just made.

With the profile created, you can now rip the pieces to final width. Then miter them to fit around the case and glue the pieces in place.

FINAL DETAILS. Before inserting the clock into the recess, I gave the case a couple coats of finish and applied adhesive-backed felt to the bottom. (For sources, turn to page 98.) In order to dress up the compartment, I lined the inside with felt as well (Figure 13).

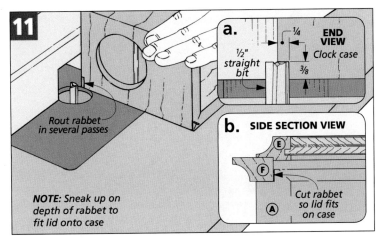

11 Rout rabbet in several passes

a. ½" straight bit / END VIEW / Clock case / ¼ / ⅜

b. SIDE SECTION VIEW / E / F / A / Cut rabbet so lid fits on case

NOTE: Sneak up on depth of rabbet to fit lid onto case

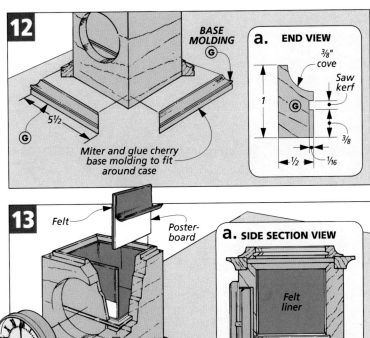

12 BASE MOLDING (G)

5½ / G

Miter and glue cherry base molding to fit around case

a. END VIEW / ⅜" cove / Saw kerf / 1 / (G) / ⅜ / ½ / 1/16

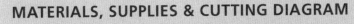

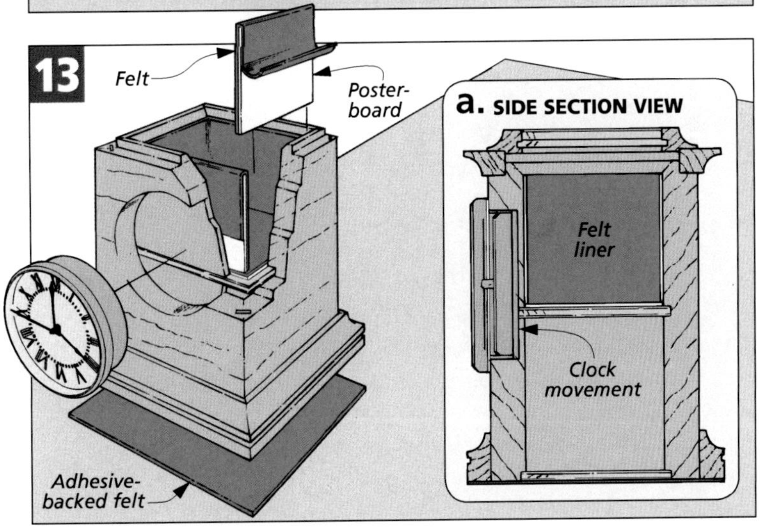

13 Felt / Poster-board

a. SIDE SECTION VIEW / Felt liner / Clock movement

Adhesive-backed felt

MATERIALS, SUPPLIES & CUTTING DIAGRAM

A Sides (4) ¾ x 6½ - 4½
B Splines (4) ⅛ x 6½ - ⅜
C Case Panels (2) ¼ ply. - 3¼ x 3¼
D Lid Panels (2) ¼ ply. - 3¼ x 3¼
E Upper Molding (4) ½ x ¾ - 4½
F Lower Molding (4) ½ x ⅞ - 5½
G Base Molding (4) ½ x 1 - 5½
• Adhesive-backed Felt
• Posterboard
• 3½"-dia. Quartz Movement

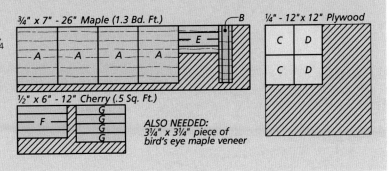

¾" x 7" - 26" Maple (1.3 Bd. Ft.) / B / E / A — A — A — A

½" x 6" - 12" Cherry (.5 Sq. Ft.) / F / G / G / G / G

ALSO NEEDED: 3¼" x 3¼" piece of bird's eye maple veneer

¼" - 12"x 12" Plywood / C / D / C / D

Three-Tier In-Box

Identical trays make this stylish desk organizer go together quickly. And the joinery lets you show off your woodworking skills.

Getting organized is not always easy. But whether you're organizing letters, mail, or other papers, this set of desktop trays will help you get the job done while adding flair to your office area, as well.

The in-box is made around a simple frame. The upper tray is fixed to the frame, and the bottom trays slide out on wood guides.

Even though the project is small, it's big on woodworking details.

Miter joints reinforced with contrasting splines make the rounded corners of the frame and trays stand out. Plus, the contoured cutouts on each tray are easily shaped and add to the look.

MATERIALS, SUPPLIES & CUTTING DIAGRAM

A	Frame Sides (4)	½ x 2 - 9	E	Tray Fronts/Backs (6)	½ x 2½ - 10	•	(4) #8 x 1" Fh Brass Woodscrews
B	Bottom Rails (2)	½ x 2 - 11⅛	F	Tray Sides (6)	½ x 2½ - 13	•	(8) ³⁄₁₆" Flat Brass Washers
C	Top Rails (2)	½ x 2 - 12	G	Tray Bottoms (3)	¼ ply. - 9½ x 12½	•	(8) #8 x ½" Fh Brass Woodscrews
D	Tray Guides (4)	½ x ½ - 12⅛				•	(4) ½"-dia. Cork Pads

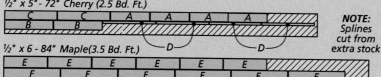

½" x 5"- 72" Cherry (2.5 Bd. Ft.)

NOTE: Splines cut from extra stock

½" x 6 - 84" Maple (3.5 Bd. Ft.)

¼" - 12" x 48" Maple Plywood

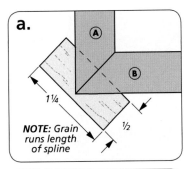

a.

1¼

½

NOTE: Grain runs length of spline

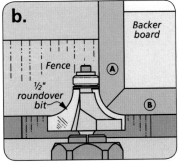

b.

Backer board

Ⓐ

Fence

½" roundover bit

Ⓑ

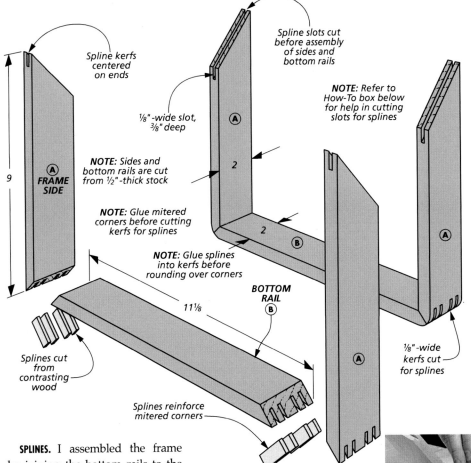

Spline kerfs centered on ends

9

Ⓐ **FRAME SIDE**

⅛"-wide slot, ⅜" deep

NOTE: Sides and bottom rails are cut from ½"-thick stock

NOTE: Glue mitered corners before cutting kerfs for splines

NOTE: Glue splines into kerfs before rounding over corners

Splines cut from contrasting wood

11⅛

Splines reinforce mitered corners

Spline slots cut before assembly of sides and bottom rails

NOTE: Refer to How-To box below for help in cutting slots for splines

Ⓐ

2

Ⓑ

2

Ⓐ

BOTTOM RAIL Ⓑ

Ⓐ

Ⓐ

⅛"-wide kerfs cut for splines

FRAME FIRST

For a project like this, I like to build the frame first and then size the trays to fit. The frame consists of two U-shaped assemblies connected by a pair of top rails. Each joint is reinforced with contrasting splines. Guides are added later for the lower two trays to ride on.

SIZING WORKPIECES. After the pieces for the frame are ripped to width, you can miter or bevel each piece to final length. You'll need to cut the slot for the cross-grain spline in the mitered corners now. A commercial tenoning jig will make short work of these slots. Or you can build a simple jig to cut the slots. There's more information in the How-To box below.

SPLINES. I assembled the frame by joining the bottom rails to the uprights first. I added glue to the mitered ends and just held them together by hand until the glue set up on each corner.

After gluing up each U-shaped assembly, I used a small jig on the table saw to cut the kerfs for the contrasting splines (right photo). You can read more about this jig in Shop Notebook on page 54.

Once the kerfs are cut, you can glue the splines in place at each of the corners (detail 'a'). When the glue is dry, use a hand saw and

chisel to trim them flush with the bottom rails and sides. Then round over the joints on all four corners of the frame with a ½" roundover bit in the router table (detail 'b'). A backer board behind each cut will reduce chipping and tearout as the workpiece passes over the bit.

On the next page, you'll find a couple more pieces to add to the frame of the in-box before it's ready for the contrasting trays.

Splined Miters. Kerfs for the splines in the frame and tray will be spaced evenly with this jig (page 54).

How-To: Mitered Slot

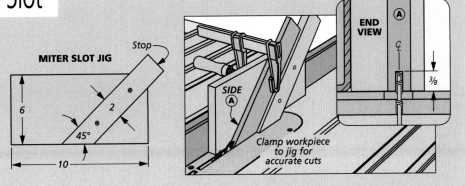

To cut the slots in the mitered corners of the frame side pieces, I made the simple jig shown here. It's nothing more than a plywood fence with an angled stop to support the sides as you cut the slots.

I cut the plywood fence as you see in the drawing at right. Then I attached the stop with screws.

MITER SLOT JIG

Stop

6

2

45°

10

SIDE Ⓐ

Clamp workpiece to jig for accurate cuts

END VIEW Ⓐ

⅜

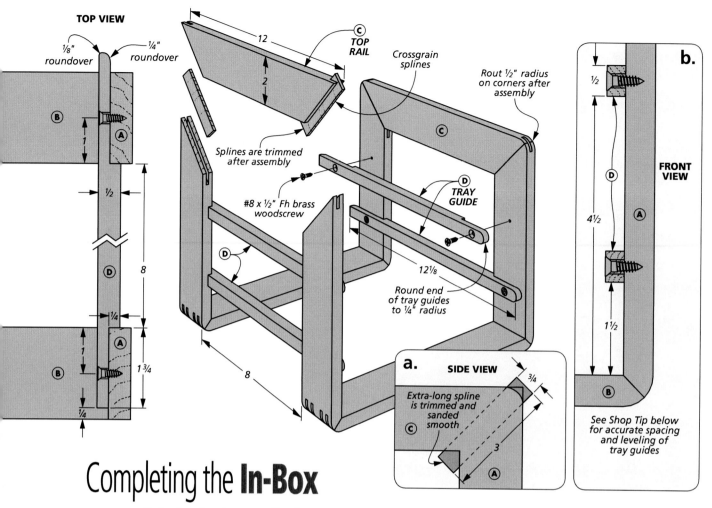

TOP VIEW

1/8" roundover · 1/4" roundover

TOP RAIL · 12 · 2

Crossgrain splines

Rout 1/2" radius on corners after assembly

Splines are trimmed after assembly

#8 x 1/2" Fh brass woodscrew

TRAY GUIDE

12 1/8

Round end of tray guides to 1/4" radius

8 · 8

1 · 1/2 · 8 · 1/4 · 1 · 1 3/4 · 1/4

a. SIDE VIEW

Extra-long spline is trimmed and sanded smooth

3/4 · 3

b. FRONT VIEW

1/2 · 4 1/2 · 1 1/2

See Shop Tip below for accurate spacing and leveling of tray guides

Completing the **In-Box**

In the drawing above, you'll see how two rails on the top join the U-shaped frames. After it's glued up, you can add the tray guides. Then three trays will complete the job.

TOP RAILS. Here again, the top rails on the frame are joined to the sides with splined miters. These splines run through the joint and are cut across the grain. Cut the splines long, glue them in place, and use a coping saw to trim the corners (detail 'a'). After sanding them, round the corners of the assembly.

TRAY GUIDES. The final step for the frame is to add the tray guides. Each guide is rabbeted on the ends to fit snugly between the frame sides, as shown in the Top View.

You can learn how to fit the guides to the frame in the Shop Tip at left. Once the guides are shaped, you can round over the front end of each guide with sandpaper, as shown in the drawing above. The back end can be rounded on the router table. I used spacers to position the guides (Shop Tip at left).

ADD THE TRAYS

Three trays complete the in-box. While the trays are all the same size, the upper one is screwed in place whereas the lower two ride on the guides you just added. I made cut-outs on the front of all three trays for easy access to the contents.

TRAYS. Like the frame, the trays are built with contrasting splined miters and are rounded over at each corner. Once you have the

Shop Tip: Fitting Tray Guides

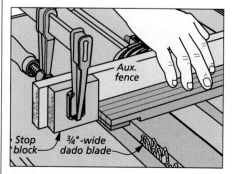

Cutting the Ends. Cut the rabbets on both ends of the tray guide blank first for uniform length. Then rip individual guides free.

Aux. fence

Stop block · 3/4"-wide dado blade

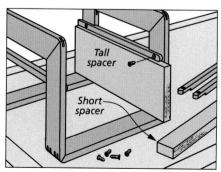

Positioning Guides. A spacer positions the top guide as it's screwed to the frame. Cut it down for the lower guide.

Tall spacer

Short spacer

blanks for the tray fronts, backs, and sides ripped to width, you can miter them to final length.

HAND CUTOUTS. Before assembling the trays, you'll need to take care of a couple of details. First, I shaped the cutouts on the front of the trays. I drilled the inside corners with a Forstner bit and cut out the rest of the waste on the band saw (detail 'c'). Then you can smooth the curves with sandpaper.

PREDRILL. Now drill countersunk holes in the sides of the upper tray, as shown in the drawing at right. This will make assembly easier.

CUT GROOVES. I cut the grooves for the plywood tray bottoms next (drawing in lower right margin). With the bottoms cut to size, you can assemble the trays using band clamps to pull the corners tight.

SPLINES. The kerfs for the splines that reinforce the corners of the trays are cut on the same jig you used earlier. Although the trays are wider than the frame, the kerfs are positioned the same distance from the top and bottom edge of each tray. Just position the trays in the jig, as shown in Shop Notebook on page 54, rotating the tray to cut the kerfs in each side. After the splines are cut and glued in, trim them and round over the corners (detail 'b').

TRAY SLIDES. The bottom two trays have grooves cut in the sides to fit over the guides, as you can see in detail 'a.' The grooves are centered on each tray side. To cut the grooves, I installed a ½"-diameter straight bit in my router table and positioned the router table fence to center the bit on the workpiece.

The grooves are stopped ⅝" from the front of the tray (detail 'a'). A stop block clamped to the router table fence will keep you from cutting the groove too far.

TOP TRAY. The top tray is simply screwed to the frame with washers between the tray and the frame to match the gap in the lower trays. Spacers laid on the middle tray locate the top while you attach it to the frame (main drawing above).

FINISH. I added a clear finish to all the surfaces but the guides and grooves. A little wax on these areas helps the trays slide easily. Finally, attach cork pads on the bottom, and you'll have a handy place to store papers at home or in the office.

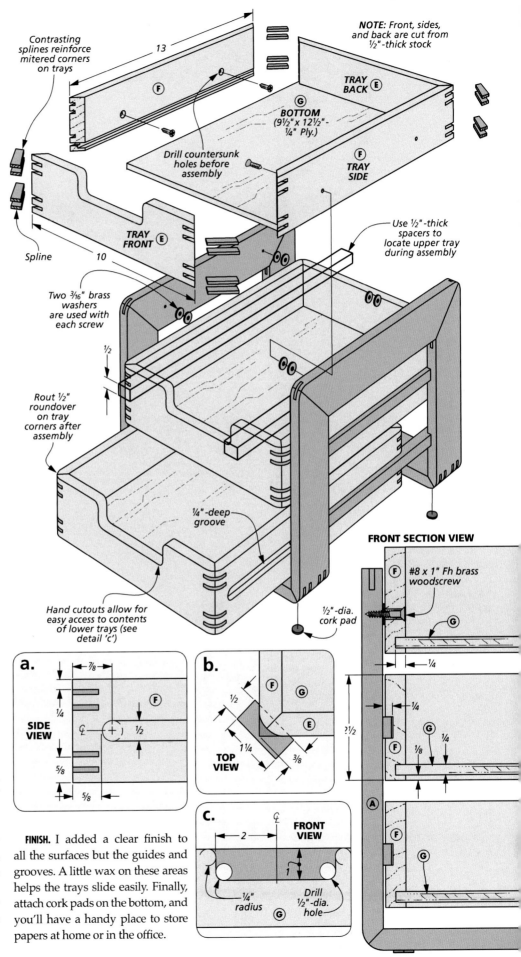

NOTE: Front, sides, and back are cut from ½"-thick stock

Contrasting splines reinforce mitered corners on trays

TRAY BACK (E)

BOTTOM (9½" x 12½"-¼" Ply.)

TRAY SIDE (F)

Drill countersunk holes before assembly

TRAY FRONT (E)

Spline

Two 3/16" brass washers are used with each screw

Use ½"-thick spacers to locate upper tray during assembly

Rout ½" roundover on tray corners after assembly

¼"-deep groove

Hand cutouts allow for easy access to contents of lower trays (see detail 'c')

½"-dia. cork pad

FRONT SECTION VIEW

#8 x 1" Fh brass woodscrew

a.
SIDE VIEW

b.
TOP VIEW

c.
FRONT VIEW
¼" radius
Drill ½"-dia. hole

Desktop
Message Center

This organizer is small in size but big in function. Its compact storage compartments keep all your desktop items in one convenient place.

Trying to keep things organized near the phone or on my desk is a real challenge. It seems I'm always looking for a pen or pencil, some paper to write on, or an address or phone number. So I designed the message center you see in the photo above to help keep the things I use most often within easy reach.

This message center is compact. But don't let the size fool you. Just lift the lid and it's full of storage. The inside compartments are designed to make it easy to find items you use every day. There's a card file to keep addresses and phone numbers at your fingertips. And a spring-loaded note dispenser lets you quickly grab a self-adhesive note whenever you need one.

The lid of the message center doubles as a writing surface when it's closed. And a trough in the back provides a place to hold envelopes and mail. There's even a tray on top to keep a pen or pencil handy for quickly jotting down notes and messages.

Construction Details

OVERALL DIMENSIONS:
12" W x 9 1/2" D x 5 3/8" H

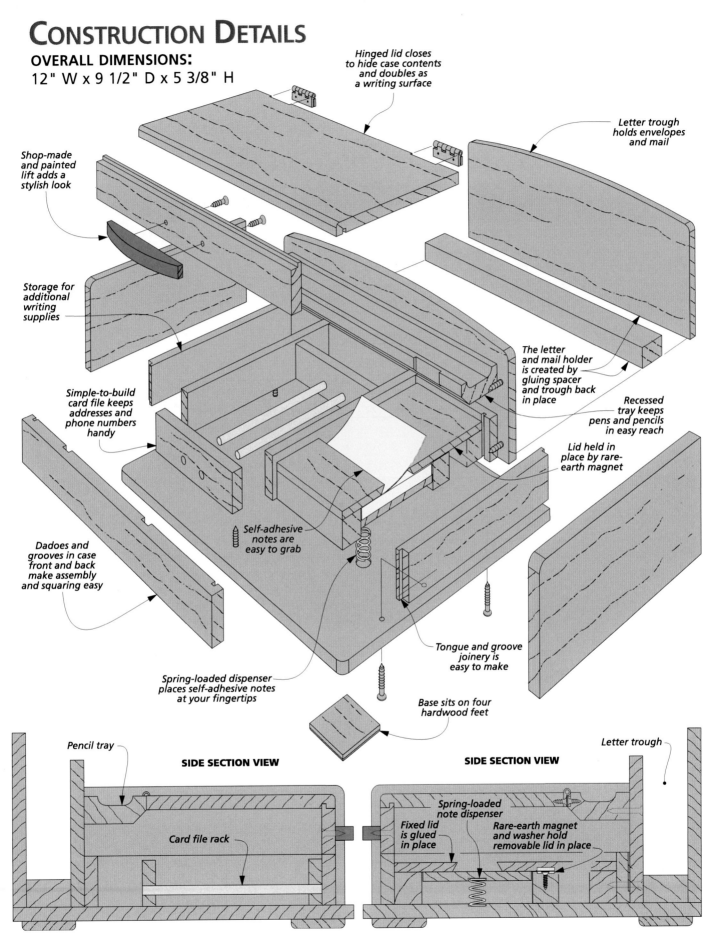

Hinged lid closes to hide case contents and doubles as a writing surface

Letter trough holds envelopes and mail

Shop-made and painted lift adds a stylish look

Storage for additional writing supplies

Simple-to-build card file keeps addresses and phone numbers handy

The letter and mail holder is created by gluing spacer and trough back in place

Recessed tray keeps pens and pencils in easy reach

Lid held in place by rare-earth magnet

Dadoes and grooves in case front and back make assembly and squaring easy

Self-adhesive notes are easy to grab

Spring-loaded dispenser places self-adhesive notes at your fingertips

Tongue and groove joinery is easy to make

Base sits on four hardwood feet

Pencil tray

SIDE SECTION VIEW

Card file rack

SIDE SECTION VIEW

Spring-loaded note dispenser

Fixed lid is glued in place

Rare-earth magnet and washer hold removable lid in place

Letter trough

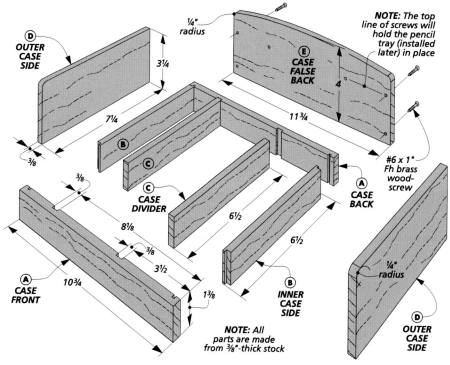

OUTER CASE SIDE — D
3¼
¼" radius
7¼
⅜
B
C
CASE DIVIDER
C
6½
8⅛
⅜
⅜
3½
A CASE FRONT
10¾
1⅜
6½
INNER CASE SIDE — B
CASE FALSE BACK — E
4
11¾
NOTE: The top line of screws will hold the pencil tray (installed later) in place
A CASE BACK
#6 x 1" Fh brass wood-screw
¼" radius
D OUTER CASE SIDE

NOTE: All parts are made from ⅜"-thick stock

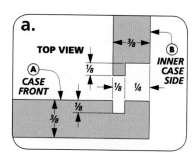

a.
TOP VIEW
⅜
A CASE FRONT
B INNER CASE SIDE
⅛
⅛ ¼
⅛
⅜

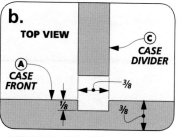

b.
TOP VIEW
A CASE FRONT
C CASE DIVIDER
⅛
⅜
⅜

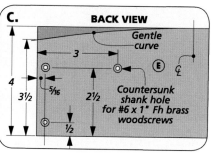

c. BACK VIEW
Gentle curve
3
4
3½
5/16
2½
E ₵
Countersunk shank hole for #6 x 1" Fh brass woodscrews
½

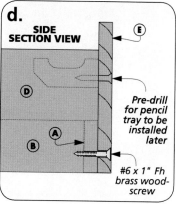

d.
SIDE SECTION VIEW
E
D
Pre-drill for pencil tray to be installed later
B
A
#6 x 1" Fh brass wood-screw

Building the **Case**

To build the message center, I began by constructing the case. The reason I started here is simple — all the remaining pieces in the project are sized to fit the case.

If you take a look at the drawing above, you'll see there's not really much to the case. It's basically an inner frame with dividers surrounded by two larger case sides and a back.

CASE. I built the case by first planing and then cutting six pieces of ⅜" stock to size. Then I used tongue and dado joints at each of the corners. These joints are easy to make and give the case added strength.

Since the joints are visible, I used a straight bit in my router to cut the joinery. This way, each joint will have a flat bottom and nice appearance. Before you begin, you'll want your router table set up properly.

AUXILIARY TABLETOP. Cutting the tongue and dado joints at the router table is easy. The only problem comes when routing the tongue on the side piece. Because this piece is only 1⅜" wide, it can tip into the wide openings in some router tables as it passes across the bit.

To solve this problem, I made the auxiliary tabletop you see in the box at left. This way, I could rout these small pieces safely. Just remember that the auxiliary table raises the router table surface. So you'll need to adjust the bit height.

With your router table set up, you're now ready to cut the tongue and dado joints. This only takes a couple of simple steps.

Shop Tip: Routing Shallow Dadoes

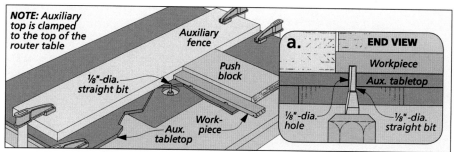

NOTE: Auxiliary top is clamped to the top of the router table
Auxiliary fence
Push block
⅛"-dia. straight bit
Work-piece
Aux. tabletop

a. END VIEW
Workpiece
Aux. tabletop
⅛"-dia. hole
⅛"-dia. straight bit

Zero-Clearance Top for the Router Table. To add a zero-clearance auxiliary top to your router table, simply drill an ⅛" hole through a piece of ¼" hardboard, slip the hole over the bit (detail 'a'), and clamp the top in place. Then clamp a straightedge in position to use as the fence.

TONGUE & DADO. The first step in cutting the tongue and dado joints is to cut an ⅛" dado at each end of the case front and back, as shown in detail 'a' on the opposite page. Using the same setup, you can move the fence and cut the dadoes for the two dividers, as shown in detail 'b' on the opposite page.

Next, rout a rabbet at the ends of each side piece to create the tongue. I like to cut the rabbet in a couple of passes. This way, I can sneak up on the final thickness of the tongue to ensure it fits in the dadoes in the case ends. I also used a push block to help prevent chipout.

With the corner joints completed, you can assemble and glue the inner case pieces together.

OUTER SIDES & BACK. There are still a couple of things you'll need to do to complete the organizer's case. First, cut the two outer case sides to size. Then, round off the top front corner of each one. Finally, glue them flush at the back to the inner case to form the sides.

Once that's complete, you can cut the case false back to size. This piece forms the front of the letter trough and has a long arc across the top, as shown in detail 'c' on the opposite page. It's attached with glue and screws to the case (detail 'd' on opposite page).

ATTACH THE BASE. With the case built, you're now ready to mount it to the base. I used screws (no glue) to attach the case to the base (detail 'a'). This way, the wood can move.

FEET. All that's left is to add some feet. Each foot is a square piece of ¼"-thick stock with an ⅛" roundover at the bottom edge of all four sides. The photo at right shows you how I added the roundovers.

Your work on the case is now complete. The next thing you'll want to do is build the compartments that fit inside the case.

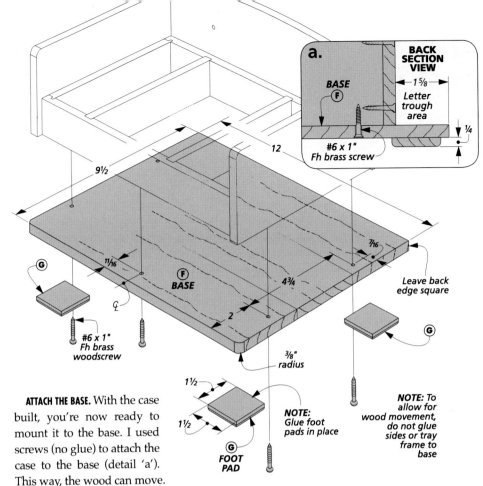

a.

BACK SECTION VIEW

BASE F

1⅝

Letter trough area

¼

#6 x 1" Fh brass screw

9½

12

11/16

F BASE

⅞ 7/16

4¾

Leave back edge square

2

G

#6 x 1" Fh brass woodscrew

⅜" radius

1½

1½

G FOOT PAD

G

NOTE: Glue foot pads in place

NOTE: To allow for wood movement, do not glue sides or tray frame to base

Rounded Edges. You can use a grout float as a push block to round the edges of the feet on your router.

MATERIALS, SUPPLIES & CUTTING DIAGRAM

A Case Front/Back (2)	⅜ x 1⅜ - 10¾	
B Inner Case Sides (2)	⅜ x 1⅜ - 6½	
C Case Dividers (2)	⅜ x 1⅜ - 6½	
D Outer Case Sides (2)	⅜ x 3¼ - 7¼	
E Case False Back (1)	⅜ x 4 - 11¾	
F Base (1)	⅜ x 9½ - 12	
G Foot Pad (4)	¼ x 1½ - 1½	
H Card File Front/Back (2)	⅜ x 1¼ - 4¼	

I Note Dispenser Walls (3)	¾ x ⅞ - 3⅛	
J Note Removable Lid (1)	¼ x 3 1/16 - 3⅜	
K Note Lift Platform (1)	¼ x 3 1/16 - 3 1/16	
L Note Fixed Lid (1)	¼ x 3⅛ - 1¾	
M Pencil Tray (1)	¾ x 1¾ - 10¾	
N Lid Top (1)	⅜ x 5¼ - 10⅝	
O Lid Front (1)	⅜ x 1⅜ - 10⅝	
P Lid Lift (1)	⅜ x ½ - 4	

R Trough Back (1)	⅜ x 4¾ - 11¾
• (2) ¼"-dia. x 5" Wood Dowels	
• (1pr.) 1" Brass Cabinet Hinges	
• (1) ¾"-long Compression Spring	
• (1) ½"-dia. Rare-Earth Magnet	
• (1) ½" Steel Washer	
• (1) #4 x ⅝" Fh Woodscrew	
• (2) #4 x ⅝" Fh Brass Woodscrews	
• (11) #6 x 1" Fh Brass Woodscrews	

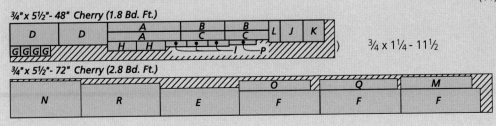

¾" x 5½"- 48" Cherry (1.8 Bd. Ft.)

¾ x 1¼ - 11½

¾" x 5½"- 72" Cherry (2.8 Bd. Ft.)

Completing the Case:
Storage & Lid

The thing that makes the message center so useful is the storage area inside the case. Three individual compartments contain a rack for file cards; a self-adhesive note dispenser; and a space to store pencils, pens, and other writing supplies.

The compartment for storing your writing supplies is already formed by the divider at one side of the case. So you can move on to building the card file rack next.

CARD FILE. The card file sits in the center compartment and is easy to build. Just cut the front and back pieces to size, and drill two holes in each of them (detail 'a' below). Then slip in the ¼" dowels that hold the file cards in place. Finally, glue the rack in position between the two case dividers.

NOTE DISPENSER. Next, you'll build the dispenser that holds the self-adhesive, accordion-fold notes. At first glance, this may seem a little complicated. But it's pretty easy.

As you see in the drawing above, the note dispenser sits in the end compartment. The note pad sits in a recessed area of the compartment and a spring-loaded platform raises the notes for easy access.

Start by cutting three blocks from ¾" stock. These blocks form the walls inside the compartment

at one side of the case. The walls create a small recess to hold the note pad and support the fixed and removable lids you'll make later.

Before gluing the walls in place, you'll need to drill a shallow hole in the middle of one of the blocks so you can screw a small steel washer in place. The washer provides a

surface for a rare-earth magnet to hold the removable lid in place.

Next, cut the removable lid, platform, and fixed lid to size. These are made from ¼"-thick stock.

These three pieces work together to help dispense the notes from the pad. As you see in detail 'a' above, the note pad sits on a platform with a compression spring pushing up from below. This keeps a note always in position to be used.

The two lids above the note pad hold it in place as you pull a note from the pad. The fixed lid is glued in place. The other lid is held in place by a magnet above and a steel washer below, so it can be removed whenever you need to replace the pad. Bevels along the edges of the lids let the notes slide easily from the pad as the notes are dispensed.

Now that you're done with the inside storage, you can turn your attention to the lid that encloses the

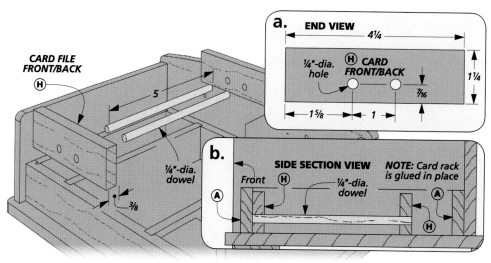

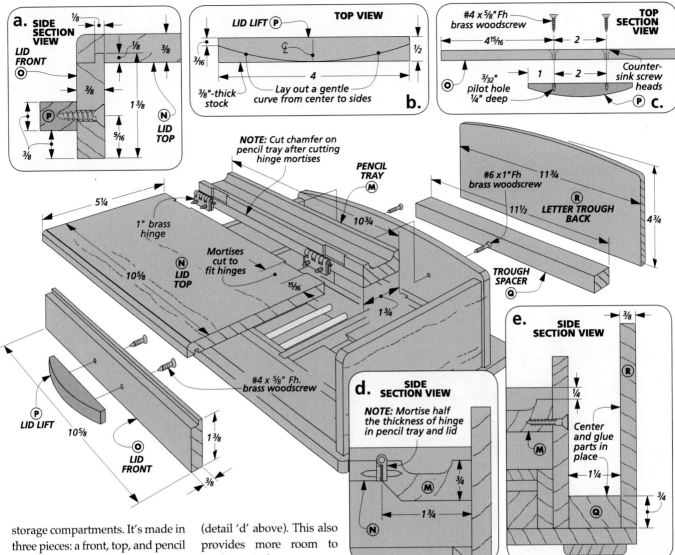

a. SIDE SECTION VIEW
LID FRONT ⊙
1/8
1/8
3/8
3/8
3/8
1 3/8
9/16
P
3/8
N LID TOP

b. TOP VIEW
LID LIFT P
3/16
3/8"-thick stock
CL
Lay out a gentle curve from center to sides
4
1/2

c. TOP SECTION VIEW
#4 x 5/8" Fh brass woodscrew
4 15/16
2
⊙ 3/32" pilot hole 1/4" deep
1
2
Counter-sink screw heads
P

NOTE: Cut chamfer on pencil tray after cutting hinge mortises

PENCIL TRAY M

5 1/4
1" brass hinge
10 5/8
N LID TOP
Mortises cut to fit hinges
15/16
10 3/4
1 3/4

#6 x 1" Fh brass woodscrew
11 3/4
11 1/2
R LETTER TROUGH BACK
4 3/4

TROUGH SPACER Q

#4 x 5/8" Fh. brass woodscrew

P LID LIFT
10 5/8
⊙ LID FRONT
1 3/8
3/8

d. SIDE SECTION VIEW
NOTE: Mortise half the thickness of hinge in pencil tray and lid
M
3/4
1 3/4
N

e. SIDE SECTION VIEW
3/8
R
1/4
M
Center and glue parts in place
1 1/4
Q
3/4

storage compartments. It's made in three pieces: a front, top, and pencil tray. I made the tray first.

PENCIL TRAY. The pencil tray is an important part of the lid. It covers part of the storage compartment and provides a surface for attaching the hinges for the lid. Page 57 of Shop Notebook shows you how I used my router to make the tray in just a few simple steps.

One thing that will help you out when it comes to fitting the lid is to leave the back side of the pencil tray a bit wider. This way, you can dry fit the lid and the tray, and then trim away just the amount needed for the lid to fit perfectly.

After fitting the pencil tray, I used my router to cut two small mortises for each of the hinges. Finally, before completing the lid, I cut a chamfer along the bottom front edge to soften the sharp corner

(detail 'd' above). This also provides more room to reach inside the case.

TOP & FRONT. The rest of the lid is made by joining a top and a lid front with a tongue and dado joint, like you see in the drawing and detail 'a' above. You can make this joint the same way you made the joints for the storage case.

Just like the pencil tray, I initially left the bottom edge of the front piece a little bit wider. Here again, this lets you dry fit the lid and then trim the front to the exact width to make sure the lid fits perfectly at the bottom before it's assembled.

With the lid front cut to final width, you can use your router to cut two small mortises on the back edge of the top. Then install the hinges, and attach the lid.

To complete the lid, add a lid lift on the front, as you see in detail 'c.'

To make my lift, I used a small piece of leftover stock that I cut to the size you see in detail 'b' above.

LETTER TROUGH. Once the pencil tray and lid are complete, all that's left is to finish up the letter trough at the back.

Adding this final touch is simple. Start by gluing a simple spacer to the base at the back. Then you can glue the trough back to the spacer, like you see in detail 'e' above.

Your desktop message center is now complete. Just stock it with a few pens and pencils, file cards, and a pad of self-adhesive notes, and it's ready for you to use.

Pencil Tray. You can find all the details you need to make a pencil tray in Shop Notebook on page 57.

Shop
Notebook

Here's a collection of helpful tips and special techniques to make the projects in this book easier to complete successfully. You can be confident every project will turn out great.

Splined Miter Joints

Greater strength, easier assembly, and an interesting look — three good reasons to add a spline to a miter joint.

Tightly mitered corners add intricacy to the kitchen containers on page 62. But mitered corners have a weakness — literally. As a miter joint hides the end grain of the mating pieces, it also relies on end grain for its gluing surface. In solid wood, this doesn't produce a very strong glue joint. This, on top of the hassle of assembling this "non-locking" joint, can make using miter joints a bit of a challenge.

ADD A SPLINE. But there's an easy fix to this problem. I use a time-tested technique to add a spline across the miter joint (photo above). A spline is a thin piece of wood that fits into slots cut into the mitered faces.

This operation kills two birds with one stone. It adds mechanical strength and gluing surface, and when assembling the miters, the spline helps keep them aligned. An added bonus is that both parts of the job can be done on the table saw — creating the spline slots and cutting the splines to fit them.

SOME BASIC INFO. Before getting into the technique, it's helpful to know a bit about the "mechanics" of the joint (refer to the drawing at left).

First, notice that the slot is cut near the heel of the mitered face. This allows you to cut a deeper slot to hold a longer spline. A good rule of thumb is to place the slot about ⅛" from the edge of the heel.

The depth of the slot can vary depending on the thickness of the material. The goal is to maximize

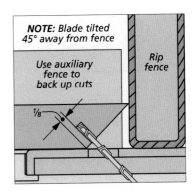

NOTE: Blade tilted 45° away from fence

Use auxiliary fence to back up cuts

Rip fence

⅛

the length of the spline without weakening the workpieces. I typically cut a slot that extends through about one-half to two-thirds the thickness of the workpiece.

Finally, the spline should be made with the grain running across the joint. This keeps the grain direction of the spline and the workpieces consistent so wood movement won't be a problem. And more importantly, a cross-grain spline creates the strongest joint (drawings in right margin).

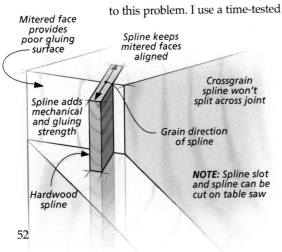

Mitered face provides poor gluing surface

Spline keeps mitered faces aligned

Spline adds mechanical and gluing strength

Crossgrain spline won't split across joint

Grain direction of spline

NOTE: Spline slot and spline can be cut on table saw

Hardwood spline

SET UP THE SAW. Once the miters are cut on all the pieces, cut the slots in the mitered faces. They should be perfectly aligned across the joint and square to the mitered faces (right drawing, opposite page).

The first step is to tilt the saw blade to 45°. When you pass the workpiece across it with the mitered face oriented opposite to the tilt of the blade, you'll get a perpendicular slot.

Now you're ready to set up the rip fence. It's positioned alongside the blade to locate the slots accurately and ensure they line up. The tip of the miter simply runs along the fence as you make the cut. For this to work, the blade has to tilt away from the fence. So depending on the tilt direction of your saw, you may have to move the fence to the other side of the blade.

You can position the fence by using a mitered workpiece. I mark the location of the slot on one of the miters and then line up the marks with the saw blade. Just nudge the fence over until it touches the tip of the miter and lock it down.

You still need to adjust the blade height, and a reliable way to do this is with test cuts. Make sure the blade isn't too high before starting.

MAKE THE CUTS. There are two ways to feed the workpiece, depending on its size and shape. If the mitered edge is long and the piece is narrow, run it across the blade using only the rip fence as your guide. Otherwise, use the miter gauge.

Just be sure to keep the mitered tip tight against the fence and the workpiece flat against the saw table. A backup piece or auxiliary miter gauge fence will control chipout at the end of the spline slot.

For an alternative method, check out the jig in the box below.

THE SPLINES. Once the slots have been cut, the final step is to make the crossgrain splines to fit them.

The spline is the workhorse of this joint, so sizing it correctly is important. It should slide easily, but snugly, into the slot. And if the ends of the spline will be exposed, you want them to fill the width of the slot completely when the two mitered pieces are assembled.

Figures 1 and 2 show how to make the splines safely and accurately. The trick is to start with a short (along the grain) blank that's a bit wider than the slots the splines need to fill. First, you'll cut the splines to thickness (Figure 1). You can get four splines from the blank by making a cut at each corner.

Next, mark the length of the splines, reposition the rip fence, and cut them from the blank (Figure 2). Just be sure to cut them loose to the outside of the saw blade.

After checking the fit of the splines, you're ready for assembly. Then let the glue dry, and finish up by trimming the splines flush.

Weak Spline. A long-grain spline can easily split along its length.

Much Stronger. A crossgrain spline is guaranteed against splitting and creates a stronger joint.

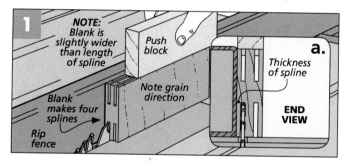

1 NOTE: Blank is slightly wider than length of spline — Push block — Blank makes four splines — Rip fence — Note grain direction — **a.** Thickness of spline — **END VIEW**

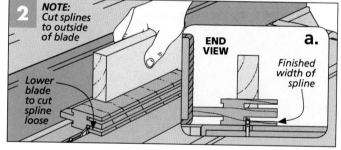

2 NOTE: Cut splines to outside of blade — Lower blade to cut spline loose — **END VIEW** — **a.** Finished width of spline

Shop Jig: Slot-Cutting Jig

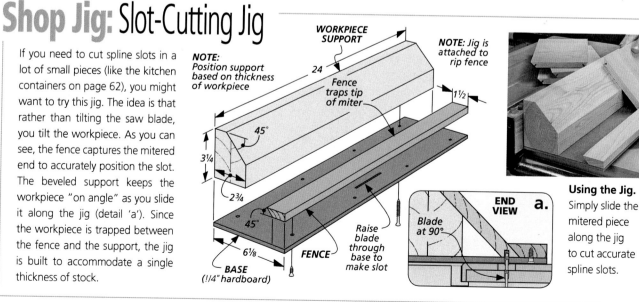

If you need to cut spline slots in a lot of small pieces (like the kitchen containers on page 62), you might want to try this jig. The idea is that rather than tilting the saw blade, you tilt the workpiece. As you can see, the fence captures the mitered end to accurately position the slot. The beveled support keeps the workpiece "on angle" as you slide it along the jig (detail 'a'). Since the workpiece is trapped between the fence and the support, the jig is built to accommodate a single thickness of stock.

NOTE: Position support based on thickness of workpiece

WORKPIECE SUPPORT — 24 — Fence traps tip of miter — NOTE: Jig is attached to rip fence — 1½ — 45° — 3¼ — 2¾ — 45° — 6⅛ — FENCE — Raise blade through base to make slot — BASE (¼" hardboard) — END VIEW — **a.** — Blade at 90°

Using the Jig. Simply slide the mitered piece along the jig to cut accurate spline slots.

Open Splined Miters

Exposing the splined miters in the kitchen containers (page 62) isn't difficult. This jig is all you need to do the job. It's simply two angled supports attached to a hardboard base. But instead of running the jig and workpiece through the blade together, as you might expect, this jig remains stationary on the top of your table saw while the boxes slide along the supports.

After building the jig, you'll need a kerf in the base for the saw blade. To do this, center the jig over the blade and clamp it down. Then, turn on the saw and raise the blade to cut the kerf.

When you're ready to cut the kerfs in the corners of the boxes, you should raise the saw blade so it's just shy of the spline. After making an initial pass, turn the workpiece end for end and make another pass. This centers the grooves in the corners. Finally, you can clean out any remaining waste and sand the edges smooth after making the cuts.

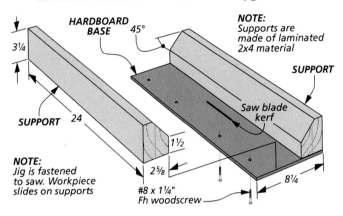

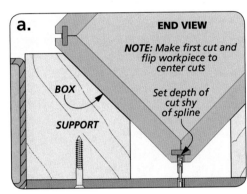

Decorative Splined Miters

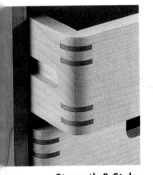

Strength & Style. The miter joints are reinforced with decorative splines in a contrasting tone.

Both the frame and the drawers of the in-box on page 40 feature splined miters. To cut the kerfs for the splines, I made a jig to cradle the workpiece. As you see at right, it's nothing more than a block glued up from three layers of MDF.

After gluing up the block, I tilted my saw blade 45° and cut a V-notch in the center of the block, as in Figure 1. (Double-sided tape holds the waste in place.) This notch will hold the workpiece at the proper angle while you cut the kerfs.

KERFS. To cut the kerfs, raise your saw blade to the proper height. (You want the kerfs to be ⅜" deep.) Then position your rip fence so it's ¼" away from the blade.

Now with the workpiece resting in the V-notch, push the jig and the workpiece through the saw blade, as illustrated in Figure 2. Then after cutting the first kerf, rotate the workpiece 180° to cut the second kerf, as shown in Figure 2a.

To make the second set of kerfs, simply reposition your rip fence

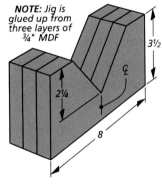

and repeat the process, just like you see in Figure 2b. Again, you'll need to flip the workpiece around to make the second cut.

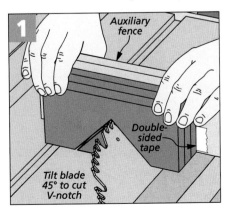

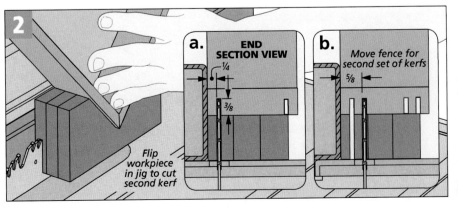

Cutting Deep Slots

Cherry accents really make the cutting boards on page 74 stand out. However, it can be a challenge to cut the deep slots in the end of the boards on a table saw. There's just not enough backing to hold the parts.

To solve this, I built a push block specifically for tall workpieces. Used in combination with a tall auxiliary fence, it provides solid support for this task.

Making the push block is fairly straightforward. It's made from three pieces of ½" plywood. Detail 'a' gives you the information you need to build it.

The base and handle are simply glued together. The wide footprint of the base will provide plenty of support along the side of the workpiece. The handle is set back just a little off-center to give you good leverage when pushing the workpiece through the blade.

A cleat attached to the back of the base pushes the workpiece from behind. You'll want to trim the cleat so it clears the auxiliary fence, but leave it deep enough so that it helps prevent chipout while you're pushing a workpiece through the blade.

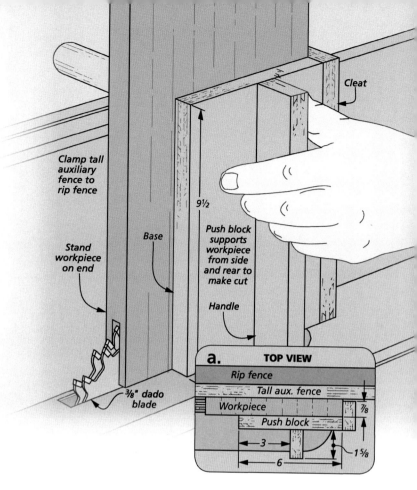

Clamp tall auxiliary fence to rip fence

Stand workpiece on end

Base

9½

Push block supports workpiece from side and rear to make cut

Handle

Cleat

⅜" dado blade

a. TOP VIEW

Rip fence

Tall aux. fence

Workpiece

Push block

⅞

3

6

1⅝

Making a Guide Bushing Template

To create the movement opening for the clock on page 36, I used a straight bit with a guide bushing attached to the base of my router, as shown in the right margin. This bushing rides against a ¼" hardboard template that's attached to the workpiece with double-sided tape. The trick is that the opening in the template isn't the same as the opening for the clock.

SIZE OF OPENING. It isn't difficult to figure out how much larger to make the opening. Measure from the edge of the bit to the edge of the bushing (Figure 1a). Add this to the radius of the clock body (or double it and add it to the diameter).

MAKE TEMPLATE. Now that you know the size of the opening, making the template is easy. To cut the opening in the ¼" hardboard, drill overlapping holes until all the waste is removed, as in Figure 1. (Or you could drill a single hole and then use a jig saw to cut the opening.)

Now that the opening is roughed out, all that's left is to sand it smooth, as shown in Figure 2. Don't worry about making the opening perfectly round. With the lip around the movement, it won't be visible anyway.

ROUT OPENING. To use the template, I first taped it to the clock side piece and then taped this workpiece to my bench. (Refer to Figure 5 on page 37.) Then the opening can be routed in several passes.

Easy Routing.
A router guide bushing follows a template to create the opening for the clock movement.

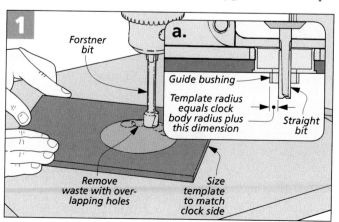

1 Forstner bit

a. Guide bushing

Template radius equals clock body radius plus this dimension

Straight bit

Remove waste with overlapping holes

Size template to match clock side

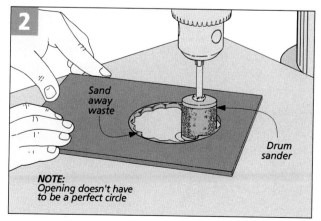

2 Sand away waste

Drum sander

NOTE: Opening doesn't have to be a perfect circle

Adding Hinges to a
Rule Joint

The door of the drop-front storage center project on page 18 is hinged with a rule joint (also called a drop-leaf joint). This allows the hinges to be completely hidden inside the case. And as you see at right, it makes the door rest flat without any extra support when opened.

TWO MORTISES. To make the rule joint work smoothly without binding, the special drop-leaf hinges that you see in the margin photo have to be installed properly.

You'll notice in the main photo that the hinge barrel isn't centered over the joint line. It sits back from the edge of the case bottom and is mortised in along with the short hinge leaf. The long hinge leaf extends across the joint line. This means you'll need to cut shallow mortises for the hinge leaves and then a deeper mortise (or pocket) for the barrel.

CAREFUL LAYOUT. The first step is to lay out the mortises for the hinge leaves (Figure 1). Start by marking the side-to-side position of the hinges on the case bottom. Then measure back ⅜" from the

Special Hardware. The hinges used on a rule joint have a short leaf and a long leaf. This allows the hinge to bridge the joint.

edge and mark a line locating the center of the hinge barrel.

Next, slide the case bottom and door together with a couple of playing cards between them as spacers. Lay the hinge in position (barrel up) on the layout marks, and use it to mark the outline of the mortises in the case bottom and door. Just make sure the barrel of the hinge is centered over the layout line.

THE LEAF MORTISES. With the layout complete, get out your router and install a straight bit. This allows you to quickly rout away the bulk of the waste from the shallow mortises. You'll get a consistent depth

and a flat bottom. Finish the mortises by using a chisel to clean up around the edges (Figure 2).

THE BARREL MORTISE. Now, you need to cut a pocket for the hinge barrel (Figure 3). This won't show, so a perfect fit isn't necessary. You can get the job done quickly with a pair of chisels. Again, just make sure the pocket is positioned accurately, as shown in Figure 3a.

ASSEMBLE THE JOINT. Once the pockets are cut, you can fit the hinges into the mortises and assemble the joint. A self-centering bit makes drilling the pilot holes easy (Figure 4). Then simply install the screws.

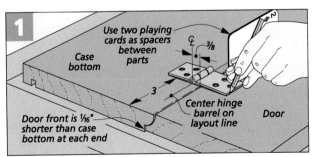

1 Use two playing cards as spacers between parts. Case bottom. ⅜. 3. Door front is 1/16" shorter than case bottom at each end. Center hinge barrel on layout line. Door.

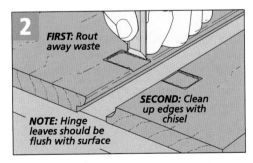

2 FIRST: Rout away waste. SECOND: Clean up edges with chisel. NOTE: Hinge leaves should be flush with surface.

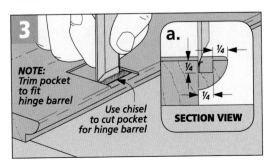

3 NOTE: Trim pocket to fit hinge barrel. Use chisel to cut pocket for hinge barrel. **a.** ¼. ¼. ¼. SECTION VIEW

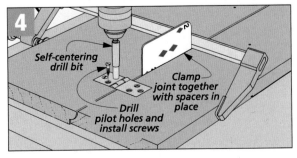

4 Self-centering drill bit. Clamp joint together with spacers in place. Drill pilot holes and install screws.

Connecting Cases

If you decide to make more than one of the DVD storage cases on page 12, you'll probably want to be able to stack the cases on top of each other. To connect the cases but still allow them to be taken apart later for a different configuration, I installed machine screws and matching threaded inserts, as shown in the right margin photo.

DRILLING THE HOLES. If you take a look at Figures 1a and 1b, you'll see that countersunk holes are drilled in the bottom of the upper case for the machine screws. Then larger holes are drilled in the top of the case below for the inserts.

The trick is to make sure that the insert holes in the lower case line up perfectly with the screw holes in the upper case. To do this, I set up a fence and a stop block on my drill press and used this setup to drill all the holes, as shown in Figure 1. (You'll have to flip the workpiece over to drill all the holes.)

Once all the holes are drilled, you can install the inserts. The inserts I used are threaded on the inside only — to match the threads of the machine screws. The outside of each insert is covered with little barbs. As the insert is driven into its hole, the barbs dig into the wood and prevent the insert from being pulled out.

INSTALLING THE INSERTS. My first instinct was to hammer the inserts into the holes. But I quickly realized that this might damage the workpiece (or the insert). So instead, I pressed each insert into its hole.

To do this, I used a simple C-clamp. I first threaded a machine screw into each insert to act as a driving ram. Then I used the C-clamp to gently press the inserts into the holes, as you can see in Figure 2. A backer board placed behind the workpiece will prevent the head of the C-clamp from marring the wood.

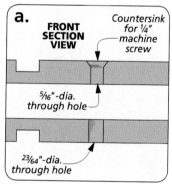

Installing Inserts. The inserts are pressed into the holes using a C-clamp and a machine screw. A backer board prevents the clamp head from marring the workpiece.

Holding Power. Barbs on these inserts keep them from being pulled out of their holes.

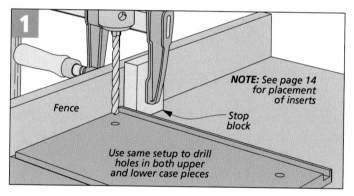

NOTE: See page 14 for placement of inserts

Fence

Stop block

Use same setup to drill holes in both upper and lower case pieces

a. FRONT SECTION VIEW — Countersink for 1/4" machine screw — 5/16"-dia. through hole — 23/64"-dia. through hole

b. FRONT SECTION VIEW — 1/4" x 1" Fh machine screw — 1/4"-20 barbed insert

Routing a Pencil Tray

The desktop message center on page 44 wouldn't be complete without a place to store pencils and pens. So I added a pencil tray. It's easy to make using only three steps and two router bits.

I started with a long workpiece so I could trim it to exact length later. The first thing you need to do is rout the two outside edges of the tray. I used a core box bit because I wanted a rounded groove. Figure 1 illustrates how this is done in two passes on the router table.

Next, I mounted a straight bit in the router to clean out the groove (Figure 2). The key is to rout down the center of the workpiece at the same depth as the first cuts. This way, you'll avoid any "steps" or ridges in the bottom of the groove.

Now all that's left to do is a little sanding to make the bottom of the tray nice and smooth. I made a narrow sanding block, as you can see in Figure 3, and wrapped sandpaper around it. Then I made long strokes on the bottom of the groove until it was smooth. Finally, you can cut the tray to its finished length and glue it in place.

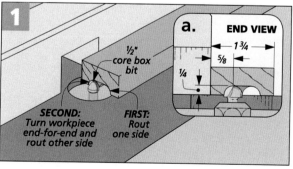

1a. END VIEW — 1/2" core box bit — 1 3/4 — 5/8 — 1/4

SECOND: Turn workpiece end-for-end and rout other side

FIRST: Rout one side

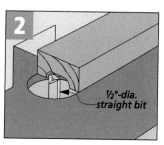

2 — 1/2"-dia. straight bit

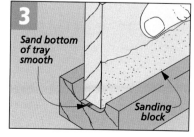

3 — Sand bottom of tray smooth — Sanding block

Keyed Mortise & Tenons

Make tight, attractive, and strong joints the old-fashioned way — without a drop of glue.

Sometimes called "tusk" tenons, keyed mortise and tenons are the original knock-down joinery for furniture projects. A wedge-shaped "key" holds a tenon in place for sturdy construction (photo above). Then as the seasons change, you can tighten up a loose joint with a tap on the wedge. With another small tap, you can remove the key to take the joint apart.

It's not difficult to add keyed mortise and tenon joints to the quilt rack on page 24. But there are a few things you should know.

CAREFUL LAYOUT. If you take a look at the drawing below, you'll find some guidelines you can follow to get a strong joint. The size of the tenon, key, and key hole all play an important role. I like to make the keys first. But you need to size them for strength and looks.

SIZING THE KEY. When you think about it, there's a lot of pressure on a keyed mortise and tenon joint. Especially as the key is tapped into place. The goals are to make the key strong enough and in proportion with your project's size.

For strength, I like to make the thickness of the key about one-third the width of the tenon (left drawing). And I think it looks better to have the small end of the key square-shaped, as shown at left.

TAPERING THE KEY. Another important factor in the design of the key is the taper. If you put too much of a taper on the key, it may fall out of the tenon. But if it doesn't taper enough, you won't be able to tighten the joint if it works loose. I use a taper of about 1:6 (or 9°).

Now, lay out the tenon for size. It must be strong enough to take the pressure the key places against it.

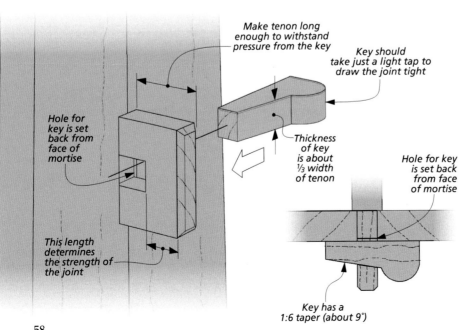

Make tenon long enough to withstand pressure from the key

Key should take just a light tap to draw the joint tight

Hole for key is set back from face of mortise

This length determines the strength of the joint

Thickness of key is about ⅓ width of tenon

Hole for key is set back from face of mortise

Key has a 1:6 taper (about 9°)

TENON LENGTH. One important dimension for the tenon is its length. If it's too short, you can split out the short grain on the tenon as you tap the wedge in place. But if it's too long, it can look bulky.

There's no hard and fast rule, but for strength, it works better to make the tenon longer. There needs to be enough "meat" on the end of the tenon to prevent it from splitting out (drawing, opposite page).

SIZING THE HOLE. The last piece of the puzzle is laying out the hole for the key. The key should pull the shoulders of the tenon tight against the back face of the mortised piece. To do this, the back of the key has to contact the mortised workpiece instead of the back side of the key hole. That's why I offset the hole in the mortise (Figures 1 and 2).

Next, I'll lay out the width and length of the hole and drill out the waste with a brad point bit. I try to drill to the "back" side, or "shoulder" side of the hole (Figure 3).

The next thing to do is to pare three sides of the hole square (Figure 4). Finally, the side of the hole at the end of the tenon needs to be angled to match the taper of the key (Figure 5). I start with light paring cuts and check the taper often, using one of the keys as a gauge.

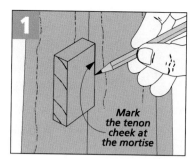

1 Mark the tenon cheek at the mortise

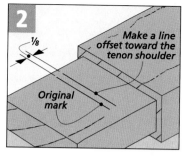

2 ⅛ Make a line offset toward the tenon shoulder

Original mark

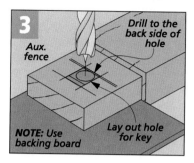

3 Drill to the back side of hole

Aux. fence

Lay out hole for key

NOTE: Use backing board

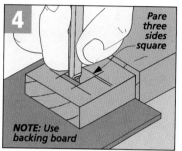

4 Pare three sides square

NOTE: Use backing board

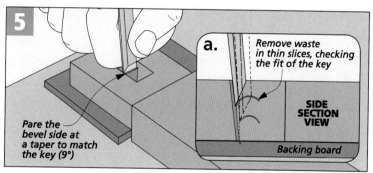

5 Pare the bevel side at a taper to match the key (9°)

a. Remove waste in thin slices, checking the fit of the key

SIDE SECTION VIEW

Backing board

PUT IT TOGETHER. Now that you have all the pieces, you can assemble the joint and test the fit of the key in the hole. If it's too tight, you can sand a little off the straight edge (the back) until you get a good fit. I like to fit the key so that it's centered on the tenon yet still draws the joint tight. Then all it takes is a gentle tap to lock the joint in place.

How-To: Making the Keys

Tilt saw blade 9°

Leave waste to sand for final fitting

The Taper. Tilt the blade on your table saw to 9° to cut the tapered keys. By flipping the workpiece, you can cut several of them.

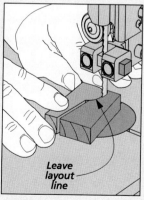

Leave layout line

Shaping. Final shaping of the keys is done using the band saw. Then sand them smooth.

Sandpaper on flat surface

Fitting. Adjust for a tight-fitting key by sanding the back side of the workpiece until it fits well.

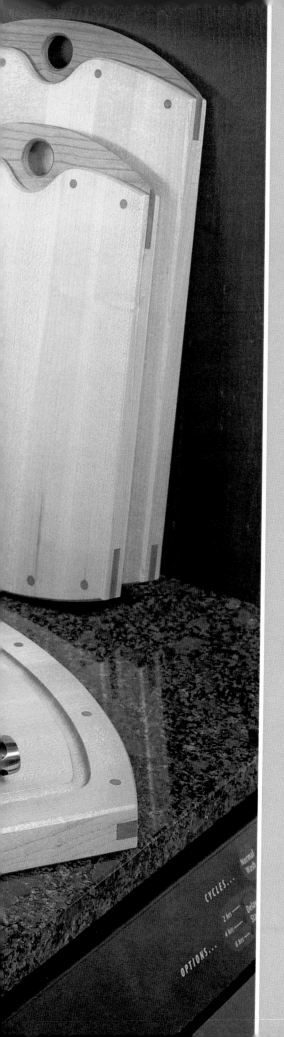

Kitchen
Accessories

Kitchen accessories can be both functional and attractive. You'll find that these stunning woodworking projects are major upgrades from the kitchen gear sold in stores.

Countertop Containers

Unique, open-miter joinery and two contrasting woods give these simple boxes an eye-catching appearance.

Knives Held Upright.
Bamboo skewers create a safe nesting place for sharp knives.

Who says kitchen storage can't have style? That's what this project is all about. These three attractive containers are designed to hold your kitchen necessities — two tall boxes (for knives and utensils) and a recipe box for safekeeping of the most-prized family favorites.

As you can see, the woodworking in this project goes beyond the basics. Each container starts as a straight-forward, mitered box. Contrasting walnut splines add strength to the joints. But then things take a slightly

different turn. Using a simple technique, the decorative splines are exposed at the corners. You get some very interesting woodworking and a thoroughly unique look. My favorite part of the project is that you can complete the whole set in a weekend.

MITERED BOXES. You'll want to start by building the basic mitered boxes, as shown above. The construction of all three is almost identical. The knife and utensil holders differ only in size. The recipe box has a hinged lid,

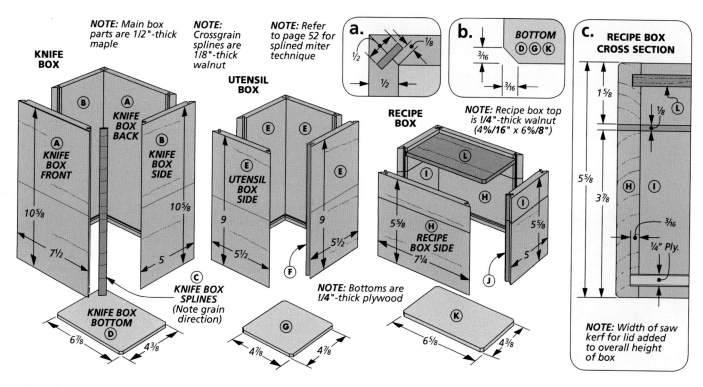

KNIFE BOX

NOTE: Main box parts are 1/2"-thick maple

A — KNIFE BOX FRONT
B — KNIFE BOX SIDE
KNIFE BOX BACK
10⅝
7½
5
10⅝

KNIFE BOX BOTTOM — D
6⅞
4⅜

C — KNIFE BOX SPLINES (Note grain direction)

NOTE: Crossgrain splines are 1/8"-thick walnut

UTENSIL BOX

E — UTENSIL BOX SIDE
9
5½
5½
9

F
G
4⅞
4⅞

NOTE: Bottoms are ¼"-thick plywood

NOTE: Refer to page 52 for splined miter technique

a.
½
⅛
½

b. BOTTOM
D G K
3/16
3/16

RECIPE BOX

NOTE: Recipe box top is ¼"-thick walnut (4%/16" x 6%/8")

L
I
H — RECIPE BOX SIDE
5⅝
7¼
5⅝
5
J
K
6⅝
4⅜

c. RECIPE BOX CROSS SECTION
1⅝
⅛
L
5⅝
3⅞
H
I
3/16
¼" Ply.

NOTE: Width of saw kerf for lid added to overall height of box

but it's simply built as part of the box and then cut free after assembly. So the difference here is that you'll need to add a top panel.

THE MITERS. The four sides of all the boxes are cut from ½"-thick maple. (You may have to glue up panels for the two tall boxes.) After planing the stock to thickness, I cut the four pieces for each box to height and rough length, making sure I had a square edge on each piece.

The square edge is used for the next step — mitering the pieces to length. The technique is shown in the box below. For a tightly mitered

assembly, make sure the opposite sides of each box are exactly the same length. You'll want to install a good-quality crosscut blade to make sure you avoid tearout for these cuts. This results in square and accurately sized pieces.

SPLINES. Once you're satisfied with the miters, it's time to start the spline joinery that strengthens the joints, as illustrated in detail 'a' above. You can turn to page 52 to find an in-depth discussion of this table saw technique.

BOTTOMS & TOP. Now before assembling the splined joints, you have

a few more parts to fit. First, each box needs a ¼" plywood bottom panel. And as I mentioned, the recipe box also gets a ¼" solid walnut top panel, as shown in detail 'c.'

To fit these panels, cut a groove near the bottom (or top) edge of the piece using a standard blade on the table saw. And after cutting the panels to size, "clip" the corners so they'll clear the splines (detail 'b').

ASSEMBLY. Now comes the assembly. The best course here is not to bite off too much at one time. Assembling each box in stages, as shown below, works the best.

How-To: Miters & Assembly

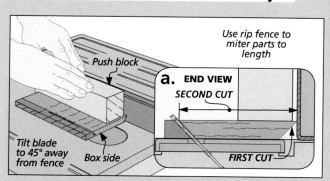

Use rip fence to miter parts to length

Push block

a. END VIEW
SECOND CUT
FIRST CUT

Tilt blade to 45° away from fence
Box side

Miter to Length. To cut the miters, tilt the blade away from the rip fence. Make the first cut with the square edge against the fence. Then, readjust the fence to miter the piece to length.

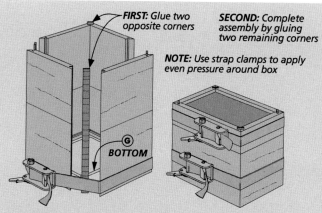

FIRST: Glue two opposite corners

SECOND: Complete assembly by gluing two remaining corners

NOTE: Use strap clamps to apply even pressure around box

G — BOTTOM

One Half at a Time. Start the assembly by applying glue to two opposite corner joints, and then clamp up the entire box. Complete the job by gluing the two halves of the box together.

WoodsmithSpecials.com

63

Exposing the **Splines**

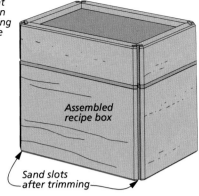

NOTE: Slots at corners cut on table saw using cradle jig, see page 54

Assembled recipe box

Sand slots after trimming

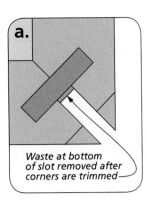

a.

Waste at bottom of slot removed after corners are trimmed

Once the clamps come off, you can complete the boxes' unique details. Each box gets a very similar treatment. And for the recipe box, you'll also create a decorative hinged lid.

EXPOSE THE SPLINES. First, expose the spline at each corner by cutting a 45° slot on the table saw, as shown in detail 'a' of the main drawing. To do this, I built a cradle jig that supports the box at a 45° angle as I pass each corner over a thin-kerf saw blade (margin photo).

The key to the technique is that the thin-kerf blade allows you to cut a clean, centered, $\frac{1}{8}$"-wide slot in multiple passes. You make a pass, then flip the box end-for-end for a second pass, ensuring a centered slot. It works well and the slots only require a little cleanup of the waste left at the bottom (Shop Tip below). You'll find more details on using the jig on page 54.

TRIM THE CORNERS. To complete the look, trim off the corners of the boxes at 45°. This softens the corners and accentuates the slots and the walnut splines they reveal. Figure 1 above shows the details. Just tilt the table saw blade, and use the rip fence to control the depth of cut.

Open Splined Miters. This simple jig cradles the box as each corner passes over the saw blade. See page 54 for more.

1

NOTE: One fence setting used to trim all four corners of each box

Tilt blade to 45°

a.

$\frac{3}{16}$

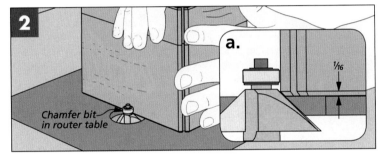

2

Chamfer bit in router table

a.

$\frac{1}{16}$

You'll have to reposition the rip fence for each size box.

CHAMFER. At your router, install a chamfer bit and ease the edges (Figure 2). Rout a $\frac{1}{16}$" chamfer around the top and bottom outside edges of all three boxes. The inside top edges of the knife and utensil box also get a chamfer. Complete the inside corners with a chisel.

Shop Tip:
Sanding Stick

Sand out waste

Clean the Slot. To remove the remaining waste, you can simply wrap sandpaper around a thin strip of scrap.

MATERIALS, SUPPLIES & CUTTING DIAGRAM

Knife Box

A	Front/Back (2)	$\frac{1}{2}$ x $10\frac{5}{8}$ - $7\frac{1}{2}$
B	Sides (2)	$\frac{1}{2}$ x $10\frac{5}{8}$ - 5
C	Splines (4)	$\frac{1}{8}$ x 11 rgh. - $\frac{1}{2}$
D	Bottom (1)	$\frac{1}{4}$ ply. - $4\frac{3}{8}$ x $6\frac{7}{8}$

Utensil Box

E	Sides (4)	$\frac{1}{2}$ x 9 - $5\frac{1}{2}$
F	Splines (4)	$\frac{1}{8}$ x $9\frac{1}{2}$ rgh. - $\frac{1}{2}$
G	Bottom (1)	$\frac{1}{4}$ ply. - $4\frac{7}{8}$ x $4\frac{7}{8}$

Recipe Box

H	Front/Back (2)	$\frac{1}{2}$ x $5\frac{5}{8}$ - $7\frac{1}{4}$
I	Sides (2)	$\frac{1}{2}$ x $5\frac{5}{8}$ - 5
J	Splines (4)	$\frac{1}{8}$ x 6 rgh. - $\frac{1}{2}$
K	Bottom (1)	$\frac{1}{4}$ ply. - $4\frac{3}{8}$ x $6\frac{5}{8}$
L	Top (1)	$\frac{1}{4}$ x $4\frac{5}{16}$ - $6\frac{5}{8}$
M	Top Insert (1)	$\frac{1}{4}$ x $3\frac{7}{8}$ - $6\frac{1}{8}$
N	Lid Handle (1)	$\frac{1}{4}$ x 1 - $2\frac{1}{2}$

- (1 pr.) $1\frac{1}{8}$" x $1\frac{3}{8}$" Case Hinges w/Screws
- (1) 5" x 7" Figured Walnut Veneer
- (1600) 10" Bamboo Skewers

$\frac{1}{2}$" x $5\frac{1}{2}$" - 60" Maple (2.3 Sq. Ft.)

| A | A | A | A | B | B | B | B | B |

$\frac{1}{2}$" x $5\frac{1}{2}$" - 60" Maple (2.3 Sq. Ft.)

| E | E | E | E | E | E | E | E |

$\frac{1}{2}$" x $5\frac{1}{2}$" - 24" Maple (.9 Sq. Ft.)

| H | H | I | I |

$\frac{3}{4}$" x 6" - 36" Walnut (1.5 Bd. Ft.)

| C | C | F | F | J | L M |

N

ALSO NEEDED:
12" x 12" sheet $\frac{1}{4}$" Maple plywood

NOTE: Parts L, M, & N are resawn to thickness

Making the Lid

The knife and utensil box are done. To complete the set, you just need to "lift the lid" from the recipe box and add a few details. The one-piece construction makes creating the hinged lid easy. It guarantees a perfect match in size and shape.

SEPARATE THE LID. First, separate the lid from the box at the table saw. For this, I have a simple trick that ensures the two halves come out undamaged and cleanly cut. The drawings in the box below illustrate the step-by-step technique.

TOP INSERT. With the lid separated from the box, it's time to add the decorative details. You can start by adding an insert panel veneered with figured walnut, as shown in the drawings at right.

You'll notice in detail 'a' that the panel isn't a tight fit. It sits flush with the top edges of the lid, but it's sized to create a ¹⁄₁₆" shadow line around all four edges. After veneering the insert and cutting it to size, I used shims to keep it centered while the glue dried.

HANDLE. Next, you can add a small, shop-made handle to the lower edge of the lid. The handle is just a short ¼"-thick piece of walnut with the front corners trimmed off, as shown in Figure 2.

Rather than gluing the handle to the lid, you can fasten it by setting

it into a notch in the edge of the lid. Rout the notch to hold the handle, then make the handle to fit.

To make the notch, I used a straight bit in the router table to nibble away most of the waste (Figure 1). Then, I squared up the outside edges with a chisel.

HINGES. Once the handle is glued into the notch, all that's left is

to install the hinges. The surface-mount hinges that I used made this task easy (Figure 3). Just clamp the lid and box together, lay it on its front, and position the hinges. After marking and drilling pilot holes, you can install the screws.

That completes the job. Apply a coat of clear finish, and your containers are ready for kitchen duty.

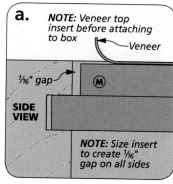

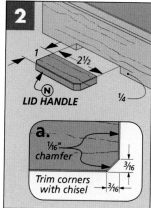

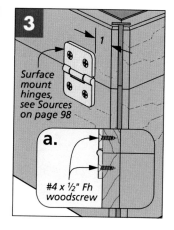

How-To: Cut a Lid from a Box

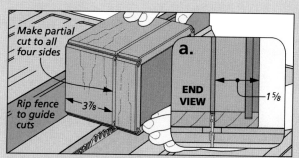

A Partial Cut. Set the blade ¹⁄₃₂" below the thickness of the sides. Position the fence to align the blade with the layout line, and cut around all four sides of the box.

Remove Lid. Next, use a utility knife to cut through the remaining bit of wood.

Sand Smooth. A piece of sandpaper on a flat surface can be used to smooth the cut edges.

"Grate" Design Pot Rack

This decorative and handy kitchen shelf adds useful storage space right where you need it — within arm's reach of your work area.

I've seldom met a cook who claimed to have enough storage space in their kitchen. Especially handy storage that's located near the work area for access. That's why this pot rack is such a great addition to any kitchen. With a hanging rail for pots and pans and a gridwork shelf for other essentials, it's sure to please the cook in your home.

It's also fairly easy to build. The frame is built just like a stub tenon and groove door frame. And the shelf uses half-lap joinery to form a strong but lightweight grid.

MATERIALS, SUPPLIES & CUTTING DIAGRAM

A	Front/Back Rails (2)	1 x 2½ - 35½
B	Side Rails (2)	1 x 2½ - 9
C	Long Grid Pieces (8)	¾ x ¼ - 31½
D	Short Grid Pieces (26)	¾ x ¼ - 9

- (1) 31½" Stainless Steel Bar Handle w/Screws
- (2) Shelf Support Brackets w/Screws
- (6) Stainless Steel S-Hooks

1"x 5"- 48" Hard Maple (2.1 Bd. Ft.)

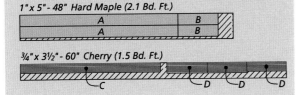

¾"x 3½"- 60" Cherry (1.5 Bd. Ft.)

How-To: Cut the Groove

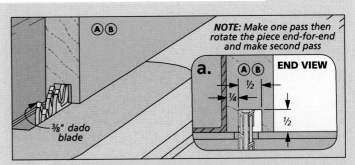

NOTE: Make one pass then rotate the piece end-for-end and make second pass

a.

END VIEW

⅜" dado blade

Cutting the Groove. Once you have the blade and rip fence set as shown above, cutting the groove is a pretty straightforward task. Just remember to flip the workpiece between passes in order to ensure the groove will be perfectly centered on the workpiece.

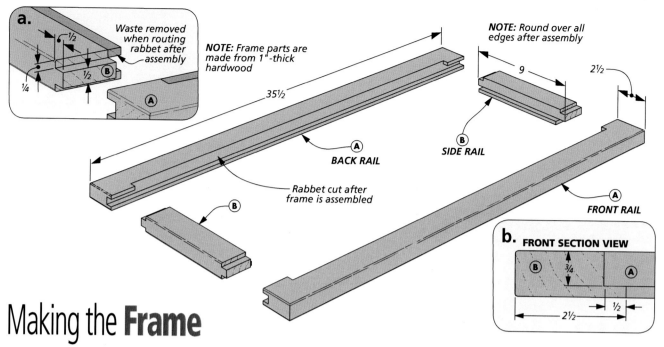

a. Waste removed when routing rabbet after assembly

¹⁄₂ ¹⁄₂ ¹⁄₄

B

A

NOTE: Frame parts are made from 1"-thick hardwood

35½

BACK RAIL

A

Rabbet cut after frame is assembled

B

NOTE: Round over all edges after assembly

9

2½

SIDE RAIL

B

FRONT RAIL

A

b. FRONT SECTION VIEW

B ¾ A

2½ ½

Making the **Frame**

The strength of the shelf comes from a solid frame, so that's a great place to start. As you can see in the main photo on the opposite page, I decided to build the shelf from contrasting woods — maple for the frame and cherry for the grid shelf. But you can use any hardwood that suits the decor of your kitchen.

The frame consists of two long rails on the front and back and two shorter sides connected using stub tenon and groove joinery. The grid shelf fits in a rabbet in the frame. It's best to rout the rabbet after assembling the frame to avoid making stopped cuts on the long pieces.

CUT THE FRAME PIECES. Start by cutting all the rails to size. Since they're all the same width, one setup at the table saw takes care of all four pieces. Then just crosscut them to final length using the miter gauge.

ADD THE GROOVE. The next step is to install a dado blade and cut the groove in the frame pieces. The drawing on the bottom of the opposite page shows an easy way to do this. By using this technique, you'll be certain to keep the groove centered on the thickness of the piece. Later, you'll rout away the top part of the groove to form a rabbet that will hold the gridwork shelf.

STUB TENONS. Now you're ready to add the stub tenons on the side rails. The setup shown in the left drawing below is a quick and easy way to make the tenon cuts.

ASSEMBLY. All it takes is a little glue on the tenons and a few clamps to assemble the frame. It's a good idea to make sure everything's square by measuring the frame diagonally before final clamping.

ROUT THE RABBET. After the glue dries, the next step is to rout the rabbet on the top side. The box below shows how to do this using a flush-trim bit and a router. Finally, soften the edges by routing a ⅛" roundover.

Cutting Tenons & Routing a Rabbet in the Frame

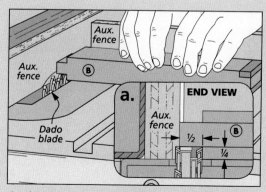

Cutting Tenons on the Rails. With auxiliary fences on both the rip fence and the miter gauge, a dado blade is perfect for cutting the tenons.

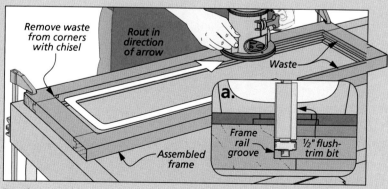

Routing a Rabbet on the Assembled Frame. With a flush-trim bit in your router set up as shown in detail 'a,' rout in a clockwise direction for a clean rabbet. Then, square up the corners with a sharp chisel.

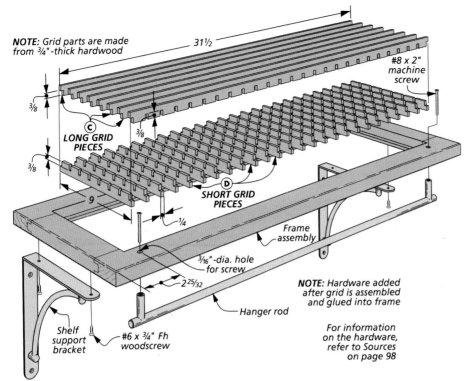

NOTE: Grid parts are made from 3/4"-thick hardwood

31 1/2

#8 x 2" machine screw

3/8

C — LONG GRID PIECES

3/8

3/8

D — SHORT GRID PIECES

9

1/4

Frame assembly

3/16"-dia. hole for screw

2 25/32

Hanger rod

Shelf support bracket

#6 x 3/4" Fh woodscrew

NOTE: Hardware added after grid is assembled and glued into frame

For information on the hardware, refer to Sources on page 98

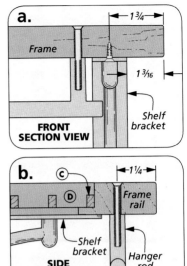

a.

Frame

1 3/4

1 3/16

Shelf bracket

FRONT SECTION VIEW

b.

C

D

1 1/4

Frame rail

Shelf bracket

Hanger rod

SIDE SECTION VIEW

Adding the **Grid & Hardware**

After completing the frame for the shelf, the next step is to add the shelf grid. It's made up of interlocking strips. Building the grid may look difficult and time consuming, but there's an easy way to cut and fit the pieces. The key is to cut the half-lap joints on wide stock and then rip the blank into strips. This way, you'll be assured of uniform spacing between the notches and a good fit.

MARK THE LAYOUT. Before you begin, take a minute to measure the opening in the shelf frame. It's important to make sure you cut the blanks for an exact fit in the opening. Once you've cut the pieces to length, the next step is to mark the centerline on the blanks. You'll use the centerline to measure the remaining notches. The left drawing below shows you how to do this.

TABLE SAW SETUP. With the layout marked, turn your attention to setting up your table saw to cut accurate half laps. The box below shows an easy way to do this.

PREPARE THE MITER GAUGE. The step-by-step illustrations on the opposite page will guide you through the process. It's a good idea to start with a "clean" auxiliary fence on your miter gauge (Step 1). This way, you can make a test cut and mark the location of the blade to use as a reference for the layout marks on the blanks.

CUTTING THE NOTCHES. Now you're ready to start cutting the notches in your blanks. To do this, you'll use a cut-and-flip method, setting the rip

How-To: Layout & Blade Setup

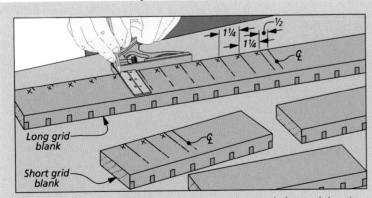

1 1/4

1/2

1 1/4

¢

Long grid blank

¢

Short grid blank

Marking the Blanks. After laying out the centerline, mark the notch locations on one end of the blank. There's no need to mark both ends. Use the marks to set the fence then just flip the piece after each cut.

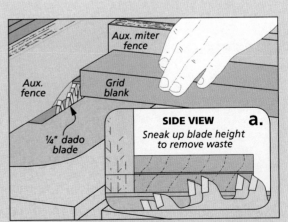

Aux. miter fence

Aux. fence

Grid blank

SIDE VIEW **a.**

Sneak up blade height to remove waste

1/4" dado blade

Accurate Half Lap. Using a piece of scrap as a reference, slowly raise the dado blade and make cuts on both sides until the thin shaving in between is gone.

fence to a layout mark on one end and then flipping the workpiece for a matching cut on the other.

START AT THE CENTER. It's best to start at the center and work outward. Just line up the mark on the top of the blank with the reference mark on the auxiliary fence of the miter gauge (Step 2). Now you can snug the rip fence up against the end of the blank and lock it in position.

FLIP THE BLANK. After making the first cut, flip the blank end-for-end and make the next cut, as shown in Step 3. Then, move the rip fence and align the blank with the next layout mark, repeating this process along the length of the blank.

THE END CUTS. For the final cut on each end of the blank, it's important to make sure you finish with a full-width notch. This guarantees the grid will go together properly during assembly (Step 4).

RIP THE THIN STRIPS. With the notches cut in the long and short blanks, you're ready to rip them into thin strips (Step 5). I also decided to finish the strips and the frame before assembly. This ensures finish won't get in the rabbet in the frame or in the notches in the grid.

CLAMPING & ASSEMBLY PLATFORM. To assemble the grid, I built a simple platform out of MDF (illustration at right). By adding stops on one end and one side, I had a perfectly square reference corner.

ASSEMBLY. Step 6 shows how to assemble the grid. By gluing up the corners first, you'll find it easier to add the remaining strips. Position the long interior strips. Then fit the short strips and glue the assembly.

HARDWARE. After gluing the grid into the frame, you're ready for the hardware. You can start by adding the hanging rod using the supplied machine screws. Then, flip the shelf over and attach the support brackets with woodscrews.

The S-hooks I used work great, but you might need to bend them open a little to get them to fit the rod. Now, all you need to do is find the right spot in your kitchen.

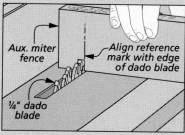

1 Reference Mark. With an auxiliary fence on the miter gauge, make a test cut and mark the blade location.

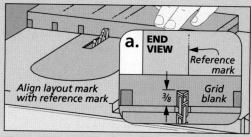

2 Set the Rip Fence. Line up the layout mark nearest the centerline with the reference mark on the miter gauge, and set the rip fence.

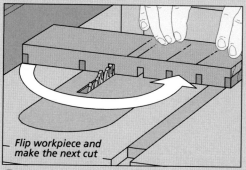

3 Cut & Flip. Now, all you need to do is make the first cut, then flip the workpiece and make a cut on the other end of the blank.

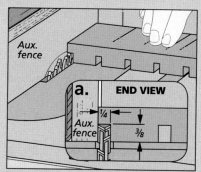

4 End Cuts. An auxiliary fence on the rip fence helps you get a full-width cut on each end of the blank.

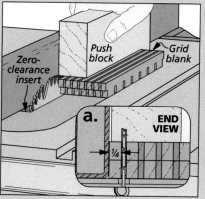

5 Rip Thin Strips. A notched push block allows you to safely and accurately cut thin strips.

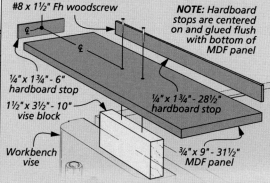

Clamping Jig. A simple clamping jig holds workpieces square while gluing up grid assembly. Wax on the surface prevents the glue from sticking.

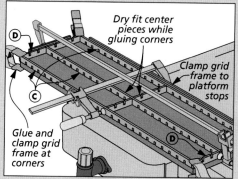

6 The Glueup. Dry-fitting strips in the center (as spacers) helps keep things square as you glue the corners. Add the other strips later.

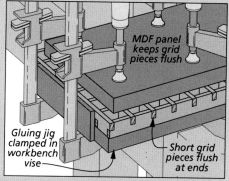

7 Clamping. Using MDF panels as cauls, clamp the assembled grid. The panels make sure everything goes together flat.

Elegant Serving Tray

The simple design of this tray will have you serving your guests in short order. And there are many options to customize the look.

Every once in a while, a woodworking project comes along that you can really put your mark on. A project that allows you to customize it any way you like. And it's a bonus if this doesn't require complicated extra steps.

The serving tray shown here is just such a project. Sure, it's a convenient way to carry food and drinks from the kitchen to wherever you choose to relax. But by simply using different hardwoods for the frame and different materials for the bottom, you can build

it to coordinate with the style of your home. Just take a look at the photo on the right.

But don't worry, all those choices don't mean the tray is hard to build. Everything from the bridle joints in the corners to the grooves that hold the bottom to the raised handles on the sides can all be cut on the table saw — quickly and easily. And since the tray doesn't require a lot of material, it's the perfect project for those special scraps of hardwood you've been squirreling away over the years.

Design Options. You don't have to build this serving tray with a wood bottom. Other materials, like the laminate pictured above, can give it a distinctive look. Turn to page 73 for even more options.

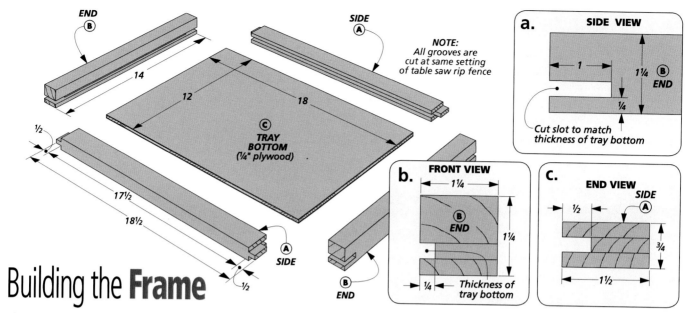

a. SIDE VIEW

1 · 1¼ · ¼ · **B END**

Cut slot to match thickness of tray bottom

NOTE: All grooves are cut at same setting of table saw rip fence

b. FRONT VIEW

1¼ · **B END** · 1¼ · ¼ · Thickness of tray bottom

c. END VIEW · **SIDE A**

½ · ¾ · 1½

END B · 14 · SIDE A · TRAY BOTTOM (¼" plywood) C · 12 · 18

½ · 17½ · 18½ · A SIDE · ½ · B END

Building the Frame

The tray is nothing more than a hardwood frame surrounding a plywood panel. You'll make two side pieces and two end pieces, and then cut a groove in those parts to hold the bottom panel in place.

THE PARTS. As you get ready to cut the sides and the ends, you'll notice that the end pieces are thicker (taller) than the side pieces. This thickness allows for shaping of the ends to create the handles. To get those thick pieces, cut the frame ends from 1¼"-thick stock.

THE JOINERY. After cutting the frame parts to size, you're ready to

start the joinery. The main drawing above shows that this bridle joint is a little different than most bridle joints. The short tongues are sized to fit into the slots of the finished handles (detail 'a'). The box below describes how I tackled the joinery.

THE GROOVES. Before you cut the grooves, you need to know the panel's exact thickness. So, now is the time to decide what kind of bottom you want for the tray. For more information about some different tray bottoms, see page 73.

When you've decided on your bottom panel, cut the grooves to

match the panel's thickness. The grooves in the sides (detail 'c') are deeper than the grooves in the ends (detail 'b'). This gives the tray's long sides extra support.

After cutting the grooves, the basic joinery is complete. Now you can dry-fit the parts to get the final dimensions for the bottom panel. Measure from the bottom of one groove to the bottom of the opposite groove. Then, it's just a matter of cutting the bottom to final size.

Next, you can set the bottom aside and turn your attention to shaping the side and end pieces.

How-To: Bridle Joint

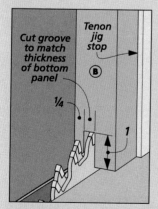

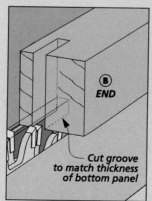

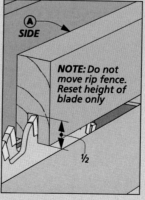

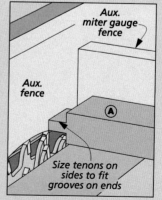

Cut the Slot. The first step for creating the bridle joint is to cut the slot in the ends. Use a tenon jig to provide extra support for the workpiece.

Grooves in Ends. Then, leaving the fence in the same position, lower the blade and cut the grooves in the ends. These will hold the tray bottom.

Grooves in Sides. The grooves in the side pieces are just a little bit deeper, so you'll need to be sure to raise the dado blade before cutting them.

Short Tongues. You'll want to end up with the tongues in the sides only ½" long. This will fit the final size of the slots in the finished handles.

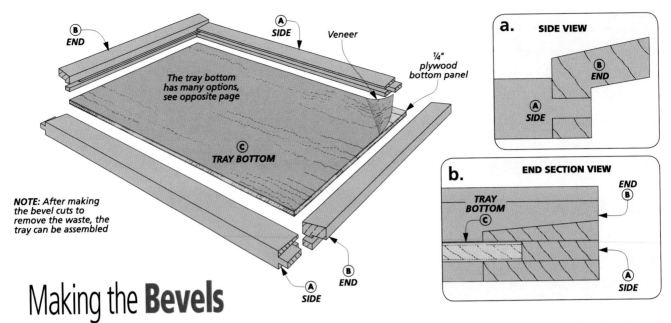

The tray bottom has many options, see opposite page

TRAY BOTTOM (C)

SIDE (A)

END (B)

Veneer

1/4" plywood bottom panel

SIDE (A)

END (B)

NOTE: After making the bevel cuts to remove the waste, the tray can be assembled

a. SIDE VIEW

END (B)

SIDE (A)

b. END SECTION VIEW

TRAY BOTTOM (C)

END (B)

SIDE (A)

Making the Bevels

With the joinery complete, you can cut the frame parts to their final shape and assemble the tray.

The box at the bottom of this page and the following page shows how to cut the bevels in the side pieces and how to make the raised handles in the end pieces. There are some things to keep in mind while shaping those pieces.

SEQUENCE. First, pay attention to the order of the cuts in the box below. The goal is to keep the parts as stable as possible on your table saw as you make each cut. You'll notice in the illustrations that a push block made from a squared-up 2x4 scrap provides extra support for the cuts, as well.

Keep in mind that you may need to move your rip fence to the other side of the saw blade to prevent waste from getting trapped between the blade and the fence.

There are a couple of other things you need to watch for, as well. The bevels are slightly different on the end and side pieces, as you can see in the drawings on the following page. So you'll want to be sure the part is positioned the right way, especially when working on the handles.

FINISH. If you choose a material other than plywood for the tray bottom, you may want to apply stain to the frame before the final assembly. That way you won't

have to worry about trying to keep stain off the panel. You'll also want to be sure to keep the finish off the joinery so it won't interfere with the glueup.

ASSEMBLY. Now, it's time to put the tray together. It's important to work on a smooth, level surface. First, glue the sides into one handle. Then, you can slide the bottom into the grooves until it bottoms out in the groove in the handle. Glue the other handle onto the tray, and then apply clamps. You'll want to tighten each clamp a little bit at a time to make sure the frame stays square and doesn't twist.

In no time, you'll be serving guests proudly with your tray.

How-To: Creating the Handle & Shaping the Sides

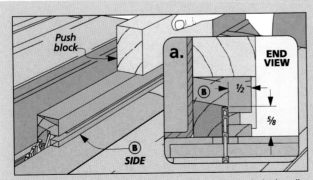

a. END VIEW

(B) 1/2

5/8

(B) SIDE

First Cut. The first cut establishes the corner underneath the handle. A solid 2x4 push block will help keep the small parts steady (and your fingers safe) as you make each cut.

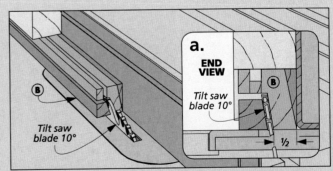

Tilt saw blade 10°

a. END VIEW

(B)

Tilt saw blade 10°

1/2

Cutting the Angle. Move the rip fence to the other side of the blade. Flip and rotate the end piece to remove the wedge. Then, sneak up on the height until the waste is cut away.

Multiple **Options**

One of the things I like most about this project is that you can customize it simply by changing the bottom of the tray. You can make it out of ¼" hardwood plywood to match the tray frame. Or how about a figured veneer that's laminated to plywood? But for a really unique look, you can check out the photos on the right. They show how different materials for the tray bottom can dramatically change the look of the tray.

In the top photo, I sanded both sides of acrylic with 120-grit sandpaper and a finish sander to get a "frosted-glass" look. For the middle and bottom trays, I applied decorative window films. A grid design is shown in the middle and a rice paper design on the bottom.

The films are easy to apply. All you need to do is mist water on the acrylic, apply the film, and squeegee the excess water and any air bubbles from underneath. There are many other designs available, too. Turn to page 98 to find a source for these films.

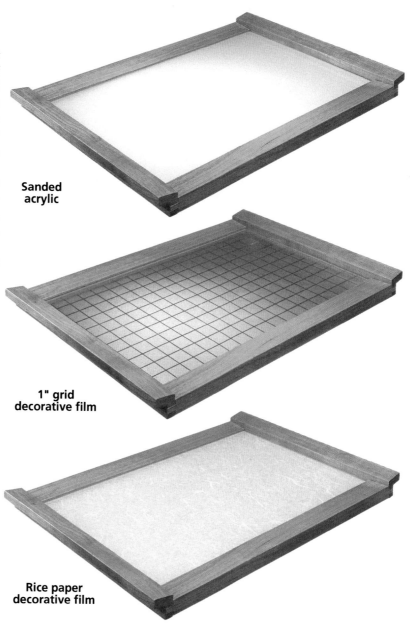

Sanded acrylic

1" grid decorative film

Rice paper decorative film

MATERIALS, SUPPLIES & CUTTING DIAGRAM

A	Sides (2)	¾ x 1½ - 18½
B	Ends (2)	1¼ x 1¼ - 14
C	Bottom (1)	¼ ply. - 12 x 18

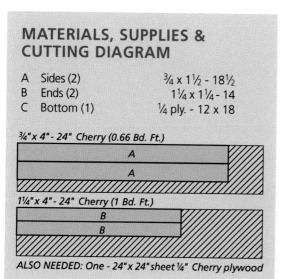

¾" x 4" - 24" Cherry (0.66 Bd. Ft.)

A

A

1¼" x 4" - 24" Cherry (1 Bd. Ft.)

B

B

ALSO NEEDED: One - 24" x 24" sheet ¼" Cherry plywood

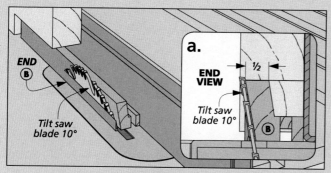

Final Handle Cut. Adjust the fence, rotate the end piece again, and raise the blade to cut the final angle. The blade angle remains the same as it was for the previous cut.

END (B)

Tilt saw blade 10°

a.

END VIEW ½

Tilt saw blade 10° (B)

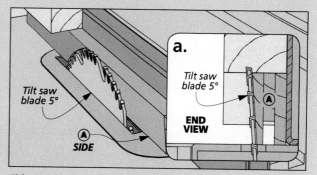

Side Angle. The angle on the side pieces is not as steep as the angles for the handles. You'll need to readjust the angle of the blade and raise its height to complete those cuts.

Tilt saw blade 5°

(A) SIDE

a.

Tilt saw blade 5°

END VIEW (A)

Classy Cutting Boards

Sweeping arcs and details in a contrasting tone help make these kitchen accessories as attractive as they are practical.

When choosing a material for cutting boards, it's hard to beat wood. Natural wood has a charm and warmth that isn't matched by other surfaces. Plus, it doesn't dull knives like some other materials.

But the question I usually face is what's the best size to make a cutting board. There are times when you need one that's fairly large and

other times when a smaller board will do just fine. And that's why this set of cutting boards is ideal.

These three cutting boards are really the same design, just in different sizes. They're made of edge-grain maple. Each one has a cherry handle with a finger hole, making them easy to move around and hang up when stored.

Take It to the Table. With its attractive appearance, the cutting board can perform double-duty as a serving tray.

Making the Boards

Each of these cutting boards is made up of three parts — the panel, a handle, and a spline. I started by making the panel first.

EDGE-GRAIN BLANKS. All the panels start out as oversized blanks glued up from strips of maple. But there's something worth noting here. I cut the 1"-wide strips out of 1¾"-thick stock. Then I rotated each strip 90° so the edge grain would face out (detail 'b') before gluing them.

The reason for this is simple. Edge grain is tighter, harder, and will hold up better than the face grain. Plus, an edge-grain blank is less likely to warp than a blank that is glued up from face grain strips.

One other thing: You'll want to use a waterproof glue when gluing up the blanks. (I used *Titebond III*.) But even with this, it's a good idea to keep the finished cutting boards out of the dishwasher.

SLOTS. After cutting the blanks to overall size, you'll need to cut a slot across each end of the blanks. These slots will hold the handles and splines that are added later. But it's easiest to cut these slots while the blanks are still square, rather than after the profiles have been cut on the ends (see the box below).

PROFILES. The boards are different sizes, but the profiles on the ends are identical. To lay them out, make a hardboard template (detail 'a').

Centerlines drawn on the template and the blanks will help you line everything up. After tracing the profiles on the ends of the blanks, you can cut them out on the band saw and then sand them smooth with a drum sander.

The last step before moving on to making the handles and splines is to rout a chamfer around all the edges. I did this on the router table, as shown in the box below.

NOTE: Top and bottom profiles match on all three panels

a. TEMPLATE
12 · 10 · 12¾" rad. · 12¾" rad. · 1" rad. · 4¼

Template works on all three blanks

Template

PANEL (Large) Ⓐ

18 · 12

NOTE: Blanks glued up from strips (edge grain up)

PANEL (Medium) Ⓐ

15 · 10

PANEL (Small) Ⓐ

12 · 8

b. END VIEW
Rip stock into 1"-wide strips · 1 · 1¾
Set edge grain face up and glue into blanks

How-To: Cutting Board Details

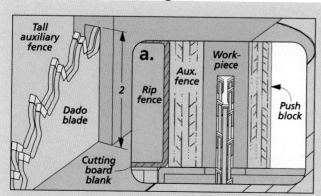

Tall auxiliary fence
a.
Aux. fence
Work-piece
Rip fence
2
Dado blade
Push block
Cutting board blank

Cut the Slots. You'll need to use a tall auxiliary fence and a special push block to cut the slots in the ends of the cutting boards. You can see how this is done on page 55.

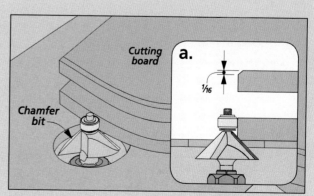

Cutting board
a.
1/16
Chamfer bit

Chamfer the Edges. After cutting the boards to final size and shape, I eased the edges by routing a chamfer around both sides of each cutting board on my router table.

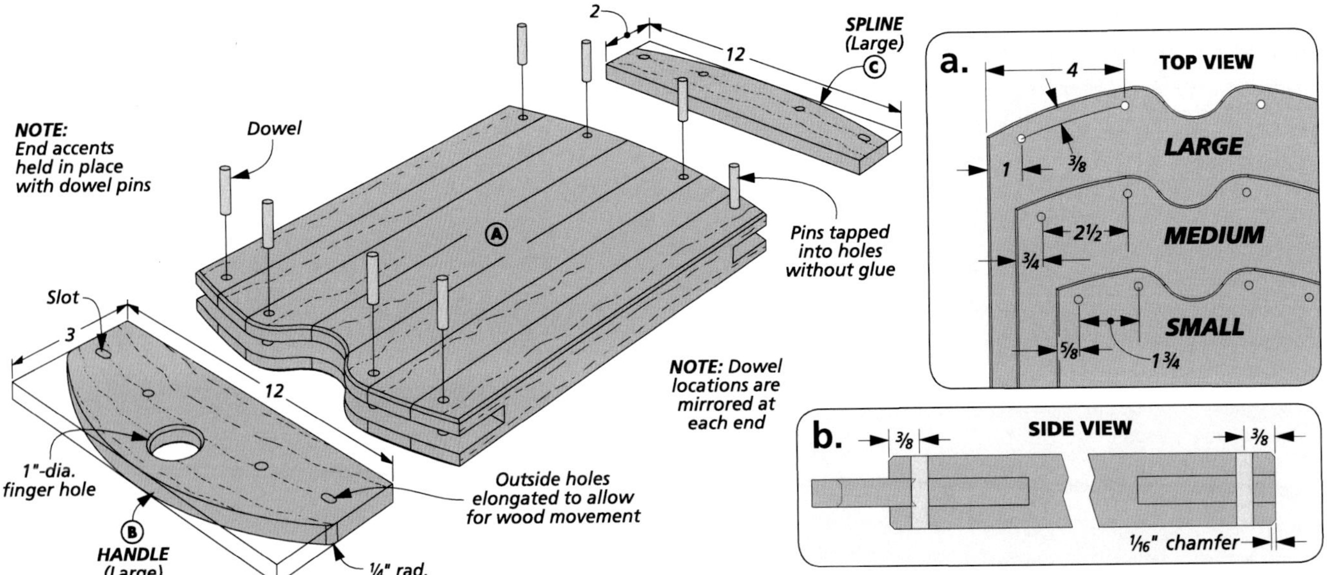
NOTE: End accents held in place with dowel pins
Dowel
Slot
3
12
1"-dia. finger hole
B
HANDLE (Large)
¼" rad.
A
Outside holes elongated to allow for wood movement
2
12
SPLINE (Large)
C
Pins tapped into holes without glue
NOTE: Dowel locations are mirrored at each end
a.
TOP VIEW
4
1
⅜
LARGE
2½
¾
MEDIUM
⅝
1¾
SMALL
b.
SIDE VIEW
⅜
⅜
1⁄16" chamfer

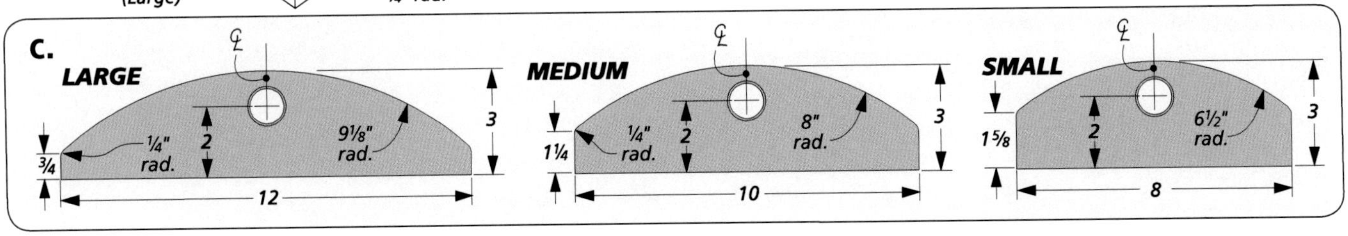
c.
LARGE
¾
¼" rad.
2
9⅛" rad.
3
12
MEDIUM
1¼
¼" rad.
2
8" rad.
3
10
SMALL
1⅝
2
6½" rad.
3
8

Adding the **Handles**

If you take a look at the drawing above, you'll see that each cutting board has a handle at one end and a spline at the other. These pieces are pinned in place with hardwood dowels. I started with the handles.

HANDLES. The radius of each of the three handles is slightly different (detail 'c'). After laying out the arcs (box below), cut them proud of the layout line and then sand the edges to the line. Next, take the handles over to your drill press and drill the finger holes with a Forstner bit. I also chamfered the edges of the finger holes before starting to work on the splines.

SPLINES. Unlike the handles, the splines are flush with the ends of the cutting boards. To get the best fit, I started by cutting the splines to rough size. After pinning them in place, you can rout them flush.

WOOD MOVEMENT. As mentioned earlier, the handles and splines are pinned in place with dowels. To drill the holes for the dowels, simply insert the handles and splines into the ends of the cutting boards and then drill the holes. But because the grain of the handle and spline runs perpendicular to the grain of the cutting board, you'll have to allow for wood movement.

To do this, I decided to simply elongate the outer holes on each

How-To: Cutting the Arcs

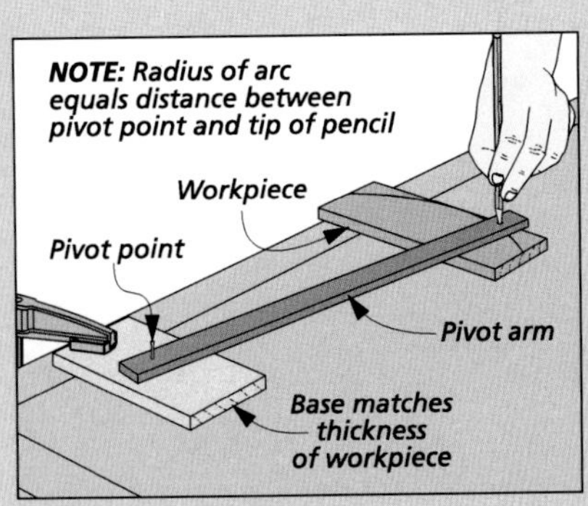
NOTE: Radius of arc equals distance between pivot point and tip of pencil
Workpiece
Pivot point
Pivot arm
Base matches thickness of workpiece

Lay Out the Arc. First, use this simple jig to help you draw the proper arc for the handle of each cutting board.

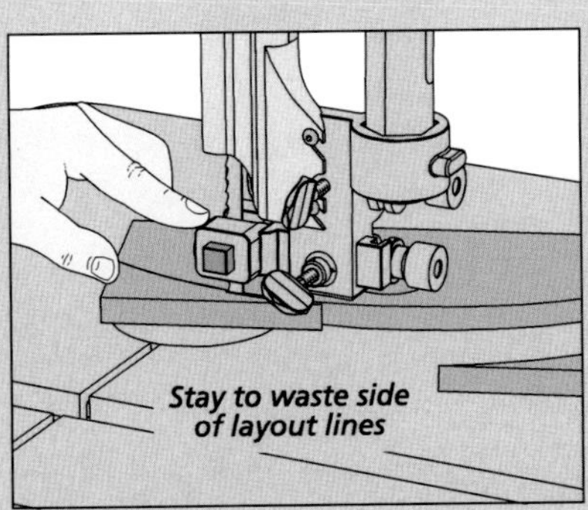
Stay to waste side of layout lines

Cut to Shape. Once that's done, cut the handles to rough shape, staying to the waste side of the layout lines.

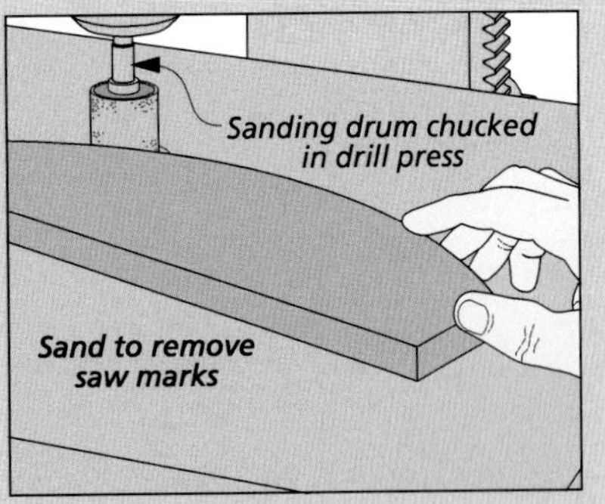
Sanding drum chucked in drill press
Sand to remove saw marks

Sand to Final Size. Sand the handles to their final shapes before drilling the finger holes with a Forstner bit.

handle and spline using a hand drill. This allows the panels to expand and contract freely with changes in humidity.

The handles and splines are installed with just a little glue in the center. Then, the dowels are driven in place and sanded flush with the surface of the cutting board. After this is done, trim the spline flush with the end of the cutting board using a router and a flush-trim bit, as shown in the box below.

JUICE GROOVE. Now, the two smaller boards are done. But there's another detail to add to the large board — a "juice groove." This runs around the board to capture juices from any food you may cut.

To make the juice groove, use a router and a template (right drawing). It's just a piece of hardboard shaped to mimic the profile of the cutting board. Attach the template with double-sided tape.

When you're ready to rout the groove, install a bushing and a core box bit in your router. I set the depth of the bit to cut a groove that's ³⁄₁₆" deep. Then it's just a matter of routing in a counterclockwise direction around the template.

Once the groove is done, the final step is to apply a finish. I used *General Finishes' Salad Bowl Finish* on the cutting boards (refer to page 98 for sources).

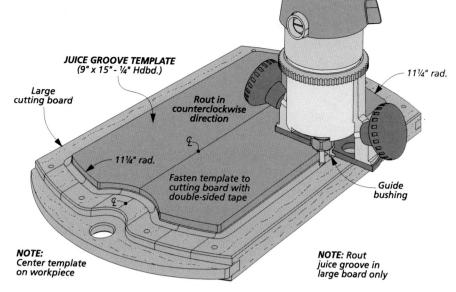

JUICE GROOVE TEMPLATE
(9" x 15" - ¼" Hdbd.)

Large cutting board

11¼" rad.

11¼" rad.

Rout in counterclockwise direction

Fasten template to cutting board with double-sided tape

Guide bushing

NOTE: Center template on workpiece

NOTE: Rout juice groove in large board only

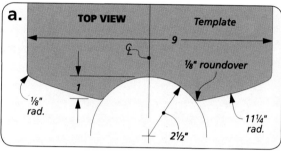

a. TOP VIEW   Template

9

⅛" roundover

⅛" rad.

1

2½"

11¼" rad.

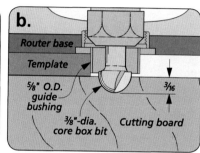

b.

Router base

Template

⅝" O.D. guide bushing

³⁄₁₆

⅜"-dia. core box bit

Cutting board

MATERIALS & SUPPLIES

Large Cutting Board

A	Panel (1)	1 x 12 - 18
B	Handle (1)	⅜ x 3 - 12
C	Spline (1)	⅜ x 2 - 12

Medium Cutting Board

A	Panel (1)	1 x 10 - 15
B	Handle (1)	⅜ x 3 - 10
C	Spline (1)	⅜ x 2 - 10

Small Cutting Board

A	Panel (1)	1 x 8 - 12
B	Handle (1)	⅜ x 3 - 8
C	Spline (1)	⅜ x 2 - 8

• (1) ¼"-dia. Cherry Dowel (36" long)

Trim Edges Even

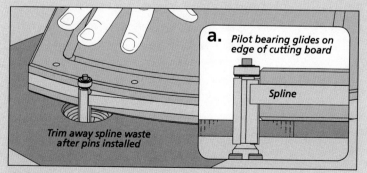

a. Pilot bearing glides on edge of cutting board

Spline

Trim away spline waste after pins installed

Flush Trim. After securing the spline into the cutting board with hardwood dowel pins, you can use a flush-trim router bit to trim it even with the bottom arc of the cutting board.

Shop Tip: Flat Bottom

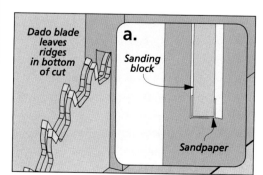

Dado blade leaves ridges in bottom of cut

a.

Sanding block

Sandpaper

Sand Bottom Smooth. To flatten the bottom of the dado, wrap 120-grit sandpaper around a strip of wood, and sand until it's smooth.

Shop
Projects

Trying to organize your shop and make better use of limited space? These projects have it covered. Not only are they easy to build, they'll make building other projects a bit easier, too.

Classic Sawhorses

These sturdy sawhorses are essential for any workshop. And, in just a weekend, you'll build a project that will last a lifetime.

Sawhorses are handy when it comes to remodeling and construction projects. But I also put them to use almost every day in my workshop.

The sawhorses you see above are built to stand up to years of heavy use. They're great for setting up a temporary assembly table. And for trimming boards

to rough length or cutting sheet goods down to a manageable size, they're the perfect solution.

Best of all, you can build these sawhorses in a short amount of time. And that's just the beginning. I'll also show you a few accessories you can add that will make these sawhorses a mainstay in your shop.

CONSTRUCTION DETAILS

OVERALL DIMENSIONS:
21 1/4"D x 38 1/4" W x 29 1/4" H

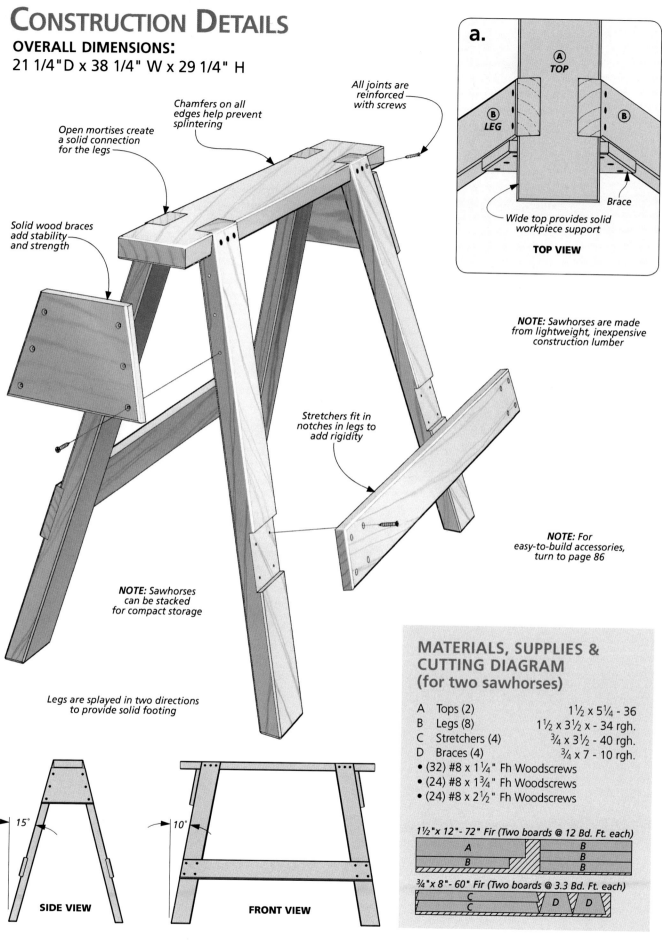

Open mortises create a solid connection for the legs

Chamfers on all edges help prevent splintering

All joints are reinforced with screws

Solid wood braces add stability and strength

a.

A TOP

B LEG   **B**

Brace

Wide top provides solid workpiece support

TOP VIEW

NOTE: Sawhorses are made from lightweight, inexpensive construction lumber

Stretchers fit in notches in legs to add rigidity

NOTE: For easy-to-build accessories, turn to page 86

NOTE: Sawhorses can be stacked for compact storage

Legs are splayed in two directions to provide solid footing

15°

SIDE VIEW

10°

FRONT VIEW

MATERIALS, SUPPLIES & CUTTING DIAGRAM (for two sawhorses)

A   Tops (2)   1½ x 5¼ - 36
B   Legs (8)   1½ x 3½ x - 34 rgh.
C   Stretchers (4)   ¾ x 3½ - 40 rgh.
D   Braces (4)   ¾ x 7 - 10 rgh.
• (32) #8 x 1¼" Fh Woodscrews
• (24) #8 x 1¾" Fh Woodscrews
• (24) #8 x 2½" Fh Woodscrews

1½"x 12"- 72" Fir (Two boards @ 12 Bd. Ft. each)

A	B
B	B
B	B

¾"x 8"- 60" Fir (Two boards @ 3.3 Bd. Ft. each)

| C | | |
| C | D | D |

Making the Top

Stability is the name of the game when it comes to building a sawhorse. Wherever it's put to work, the sawhorse needs to stand up to heavy use without wobbling.

The problem with many sawhorse designs is that they tend to loosen up after a short time. If you want to end up with a sawhorse that will stay strong and rigid for years, it takes a combination of the right materials and design.

THE RIGHT MATERIALS. Building long-lasting sawhorses doesn't mean you need to use premium materials. Ordinary, construction-grade Douglas Fir does the job nicely. It provides a good balance between strength and light weight, making the sawhorses easy to move around the shop as needed.

It pays to take a little time to sort through the stack of boards at the home center to find some that are straight and free of knots. I know this sounds like a tall order. But I've found that by cutting the pieces from wider stock (2x10s or 2x12s), I can cut around defects and

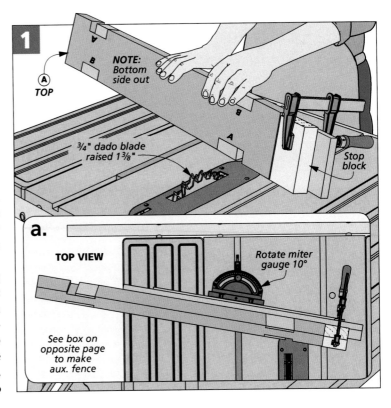

1

NOTE: Bottom side out

TOP Ⓐ

¾" dado blade raised 1⅜"

Stop block

a.

TOP VIEW

Rotate miter gauge 10°

See box on opposite page to make aux. fence

large knots. This makes it easy to get parts with clear, straight grain.

THE RIGHT DESIGN. What makes these sawhorses stand out is the way each of the pieces interlocks with the others. That starts with how the legs are joined to the top. Notches in the top form open mortises for

the legs. These notches do double duty. First, they "lock" the legs in place so they won't wiggle. And second, they splay the legs in two directions for added stability.

THE TOP. I started work on the sawhorse by cutting the top to finished size. Next, I marked the location of the four notches on the bottom face (Bottom View at left). The notches are angled so the legs spread 15° out to the side and 10° outward from the ends. Take a look at the drawing at left to see what I mean.

Since the legs are angled in two directions, these notches also have to be angled in two directions. This requires cutting compound angles. But there's no need to worry. It's easier than it sounds.

BEVELED FENCE. To simplify cutting the compound angles, add a beveled auxiliary fence to the miter gauge, as illustrated in Figure 1. This holds the workpiece at 15° and automatically gives you the correct angle for the spread of the legs.

The beveled fence is easy to make. All the details are in the box at the bottom of the opposite page.

The second notch angle tilts the legs toward the ends. Cutting this

OPEN MORTISE LAYOUT

36

5¼

TOP Ⓐ BOTTOM VIEW

A B B A

3¾ 3½

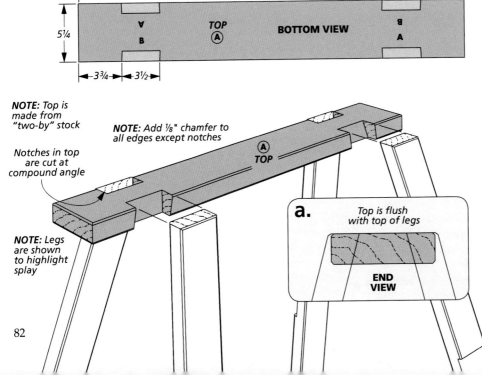

NOTE: Top is made from "two-by" stock

NOTE: Add ⅛" chamfer to all edges except notches

Ⓐ TOP

Notches in top are cut at compound angle

NOTE: Legs are shown to highlight splay

a.

Top is flush with top of legs

END VIEW

10° angle is simply a matter of adjusting your miter gauge.

A quick way to cut these notches is to complete them in pairs. This way, you only have to change your setup once. Two of the notches are cut using the right miter gauge slot and the other two are cut using the left slot. To help me keep things straight, I labeled the notches "A" and "B," as shown in the drawing at the bottom of the previous page. And to accurately locate the notches along the edge of the workpiece, I used a stop block clamped to the auxiliary fence, as you can see in Figures 1 and 2.

CUTTING THE NOTCHES. I started cutting the notches by working on the "A" pair. First, I installed a dado blade and then raised it to $1\frac{3}{8}$". Second, I positioned the miter gauge in the right miter gauge slot and set the miter gauge to 10° (Figure 1). A stop block clamped to the fence establishes one edge of the notches. Next, I repositioned the stop block and cut the other edge. Then, I removed the waste by making several passes over the blade.

When cutting the "B" pair of notches, move the miter gauge from the right miter slot to the left miter slot. Then, change the miter gauge to the opposite 10° angle setting before cutting the notches.

CHAMFERED EDGES. After the notches were cut, I wanted to be sure to keep the edges on the top piece from splintering. So I routed a $\frac{1}{8}$"

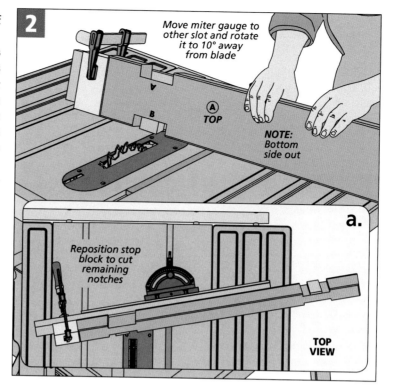

Move miter gauge to other slot and rotate it to 10° away from blade

NOTE: Bottom side out

Ⓐ TOP

a.

Reposition stop block to cut remaining notches

TOP VIEW

chamfer on all of the top and bottom edges. Doing this operation at the router table keeps you from accidentally chamfering the inside edges of the notches.

With the top pieces done, you can set them aside and turn the page to get started on the legs.

Beveled Fence

Attaching a beveled fence to your miter gauge makes it easier to cut the compound angle in the top of the sawhorse. The drawings below show you how it's made.

The fence starts with a piece of stock bevel ripped at a 15° angle. It's fastened to the miter gauge with screws. Attached to the beveled fence is an auxiliary fence.

It backs up the top to prevent chipping when cutting the notches. Plus, it provides a place to clamp a stop block to prevent the workpiece from shifting while you make the cuts.

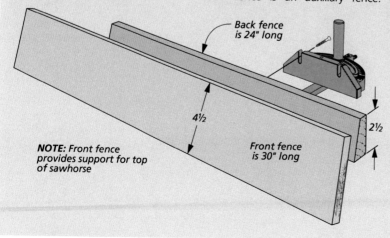

Back fence is 24" long

$4\frac{1}{2}$

$2\frac{1}{2}$

NOTE: Front fence provides support for top of sawhorse

Front fence is 30" long

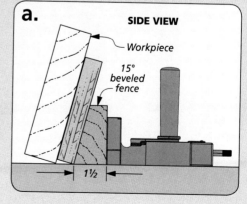

a.

SIDE VIEW

Workpiece

15° beveled fence

$1\frac{1}{2}$

Four Sturdy Legs

3 FIGURE

With the top done, you can work on the legs. They're cut from the same "two-by" stock. You just need to rip them to width to fit in the notches and cut them extra long.

CUT TO LENGTH. After cutting the legs to width, the next step is to trim them to length. The top end of the leg needs to fit flush with the upper face of the top. At the same time, the bottom end must sit flat on the floor, as in Figure 3.

The first step is to make a compound miter cut on one end of each leg. To do that, I tilted the saw blade to 15° and set the miter gauge to 10° (Figures 4 and 4a).

Once you complete the cuts on one end, the next step is to cut the legs to final length. To do that, you'll need to reset the miter gauge to 10° in the opposite direction (Figures 5 and 5a). Then you can cut the other end of each leg to length. To make sure the legs would all end up the same length, I used the first leg to help me position a stop block on the auxiliary fence. This makes cutting the rest of the legs a breeze.

LAY OUT THE NOTCHES. After the legs have been cut to finished length,

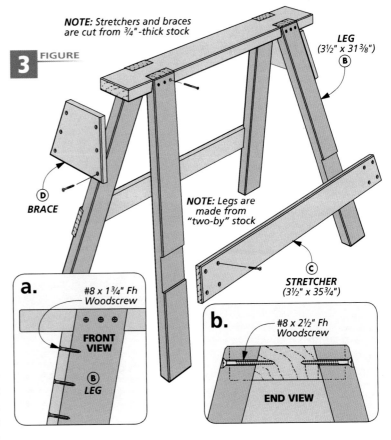

NOTE: Stretchers and braces are cut from ¾"-thick stock

LEG (3½" x 31⅜") B

D BRACE

NOTE: Legs are made from "two-by" stock

STRETCHER (3½" x 35¾") C

a. #8 x 1¾" Fh Woodscrew — FRONT VIEW — B LEG

b. #8 x 2½" Fh Woodscrew — END VIEW

you're ready to lay out notches for stretchers. The stretchers fit in the notches and join the legs together on each side of the sawhorse to keep them from racking.

To help me visualize how the stretchers would fit on the legs, I first dry assembled the legs in the notches in the top and then

labeled them to match the letters of the notches. Then, I removed the legs from the top and marked the location of the notch in each leg, as illustrated in Figure 6. Just be sure these notches are laid out parallel to the ends of the legs.

CUTTING THE NOTCHES. Cutting the ⅜"-deep notches for the stretchers is

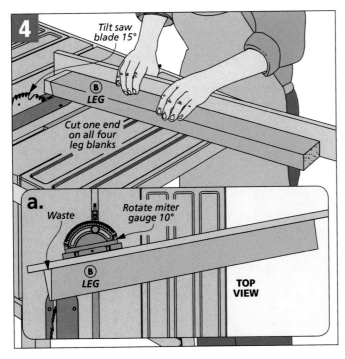

4 Tilt saw blade 15° — B LEG — Cut one end on all four leg blanks

a. Waste — Rotate miter gauge 10° — B LEG — TOP VIEW

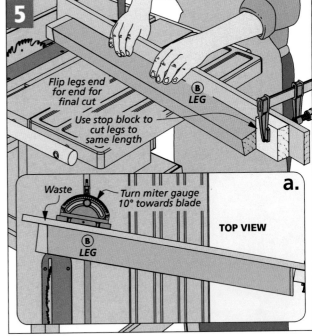

5 Flip legs end for end for final cut — B LEG — Use stop block to cut legs to same length

a. Waste — Turn miter gauge 10° towards blade — B LEG — TOP VIEW

pretty straightforward. First, install a dado blade in the table saw. Then you can use the same 10° setting on the miter gauge to follow your layout lines and cut out the notches, as in Figures 7 and 7a. Just as you did for cutting the ends of the legs, you'll need to reset the miter gauge to the opposite 10° setting for cutting the opposite pair of legs.

CHAMFER THE ENDS. Sawhorses are always dragged around the shop. To keep the ends of the legs from chipping, rout an ⅛" chamfer around the bottom of them. Then, glue and screw the legs to the top.

STRETCHERS. After the legs have been fastened to the top, you can cut the stretchers to fit in the legs. Just like cutting the legs, rip the stretchers to finished width so they fit snugly in the notches in the legs. But leave them a little long. This way, you can use the legs to mark the stretcher length for an exact fit.

To do that, cut a 10° angle on one end of the stretcher so it fits flush with the edge of the leg, as shown in Figure 8. Then, use the other leg as a guide to mark the length of the stretcher, and cut it to size.

After the first stretcher is cut to length, use it to mark the other one. This ensures an exact copy, and the assembled horse will be square.

CHAMFER THE EDGES. Once again, to keep the edges of the stretchers from splintering, I routed a ⅛" chamfer along the outer edges of

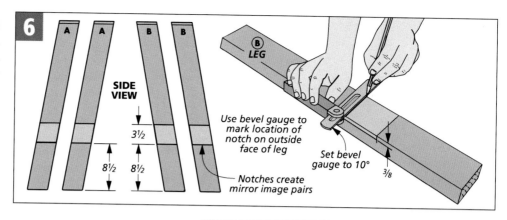

6

SIDE VIEW

3½

8½ 8½

⅜

Notches create mirror image pairs

LEG ⓑ

Use bevel gauge to mark location of notch on outside face of leg

Set bevel gauge to 10°

the stretchers. Then, glue and screw the stretchers to the legs.

BRACES. The last pieces added to the sawhorse are the braces. They're installed on the ends of the sawhorse to keep the legs from "doing the splits" when anything heavy is set on the top (Figure 9).

CUT TO FIT. I started making the braces by cutting them to rough size. Next I cut a 10° bevel on one edge. This bevel lets the brace fit tight against the bottom face of the top, as you can see in Figure 9a. Then, rip the opposite edge of the brace to final width.

Next, I "custom fit" the brace to the legs for perfect angles. I started by cutting one side on the table saw, using the miter gauge to get the proper angle. Then, I clamped the brace in position, marked the opposite side, and simply cut to that mark, as shown in Figure 9. I used the finished brace as a template to make the second one.

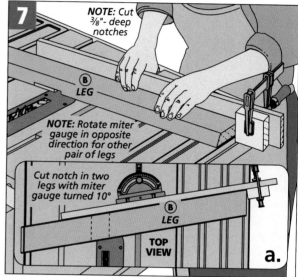

7

NOTE: Cut ⅜"-deep notches

LEG ⓑ

NOTE: Rotate miter gauge in opposite direction for other pair of legs

Cut notch in two legs with miter gauge turned 10°

LEG ⓑ

TOP VIEW

a.

Here again, I finished work on the braces by routing a chamfer around the outer face. But don't chamfer the top edge. Finally, glue and screw both braces in place (Figure 9b). You can put the sawhorses to use right away, or build the accessories shown on the next page.

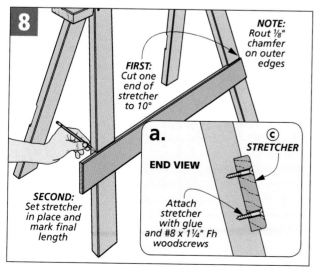

8

NOTE: Rout ⅛" chamfer on outer edges

FIRST: Cut one end of stretcher to 10°

SECOND: Set stretcher in place and mark final length

a.

STRETCHER ⓒ

END VIEW

Attach stretcher with glue and #8 x 1¼" Fh woodscrews

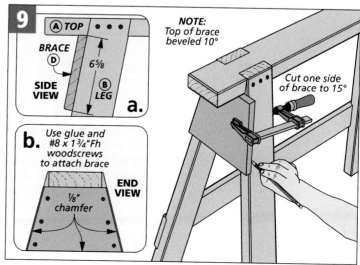

9

ⓐ TOP ● ● ●

BRACE ⓓ

6⅝

SIDE VIEW

LEG ⓑ

a.

NOTE: Top of brace beveled 10°

Cut one side of brace to 15°

b. Use glue and #8 x 1¾" Fh woodscrews to attach brace

⅛" chamfer

END VIEW

3

Upright
(1½" x 3½" - 72")

Dowel fixed in
right upright
(detail 'a')

1" x 43"
PVC pipe

42

Workpiece
support
(½"-dia.
dowel x 4")
(detail 'a')

Upper notches
in upright
hook over top
of sawhorse

Rail
(1"-dia. dowel x 24")

NOTE: Lower
notches hook
over top of
stretcher

A Few Helpful **Accessories**

There's no doubt that having a pair of sawhorses will prove to be a big help in your workshop. But to make them even more useful, I've also come up with some simple accessories. These additions are designed to make a few tough tasks more manageable.

FINISHING EASEL

Finishing doors and other flat project parts is always a challenge. First, you need to find a place to set the part (usually your workbench), then you end up hunching over it while you apply the finish. At the end of the day, you can count on having an aching back.

A better solution is to build the easel attachment shown in the drawing at right. It not only holds the project at a comfortable height, but you can keep your workbench clear for other tasks.

UPRIGHTS. The main parts of the easel are a pair of uprights made from "two-by" stock. A square notch at the bottom of each upright hooks behind the stretcher of the sawhorse (Figure 10c). An angled notch in the upright nestles against the top (Figure 10b).

A PAIR OF DOWELS. To keep the uprights aligned, drill a pair of holes in each one and insert long dowels. I glued and screwed the ends of the dowels to one of the uprights (Figure 10a). This way, the other upright adjusts to accommodate different sized projects.

FINAL DETAILS. To keep the freshly finished project from sticking to the uprights, I attached two lengths of PVC pipe. I fastened the pipes in place with screws. Finally, a pair of short dowels in the uprights supports the bottom edge of the piece you're finishing. Just drill holes and insert the dowel pieces in the locations shown in Figure 10.

OUTFEED SUPPORT

Whether you're cutting a large workpiece on the table saw or running long boards through a planer, supporting the outfeed end is a challenge. But instead of trying to rig up a separate solution for every tool I use, I pull out my trusty sawhorse and the simple, adjustable support shown in Figure 11.

The outfeed support is just a ¾" plywood panel with a short piece of PVC pipe screwed to the top. The smooth, curved surface of the PVC pipe allows a workpiece to

a.

TOP
VIEW

Rail

Upright

PVC pipe

#8 x 1¼" Fh
woodscrew

b. Upright   PVC pipe

Workpiece
support

Rail

#8 x 1¾" Fh
woodscrew

¾

1⁵⁄₁₆

15°

4⁷⁄₈

END VIEW

c.   Upright

2½

Stretcher

1½

**END
VIEW**

slide easily across the top without catching. And the sawhorse provides a wide, stable base so the support won't tip over.

A pair of slots in the plywood lets you attach the support to the sawhorse with studded knobs and washers. I installed a pair of threaded inserts in the top of the sawhorse to hold the knobs.

CUTTING GRID

Working with sheet goods requires a large surface to provide support while you cut them down into manageable pieces. The cutting grid shown below placed on top of your sawhorses makes this task easier and more comfortable.

The grid is made up of interlocking rails and cross rails. The notch locations are shown in Figure 12. You'll also need to cut a pair of notches in the bottom edge of each of the long rails, as you can see

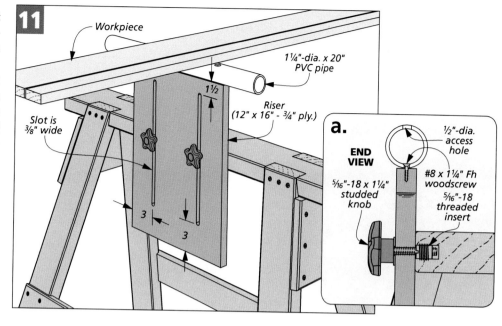

in Figure 12a. This keeps the grid from shifting around as you work.

To use the cutting grid, assemble the pieces on top of the sawhorses (no glue or screws are nec-

essary). Then lift your workpiece onto the grid and you're ready to go to work. Once you're done, you can disassemble the grid and store the pieces out of the way.

12 FIGURE

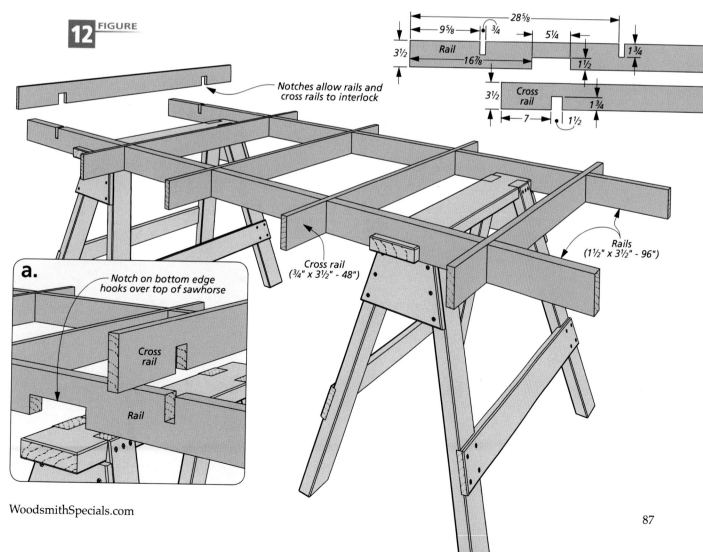

WoodsmithSpecials.com

87

Sturdy Support.
The tote doubles as a convenient step stool.

Utility Tool Tote

This combination tool tote and step stool is easy to build and a handy addition to any shop.

Working on a project in the shop is a breeze. All your tools are within easy reach. But what do you do if you need to take your tools outside the shop? A great solution is the tool tote shown in the photo above.

As you can see, this versatile tote has a lot of room for tools. And, with a sliding tray and a couple of "cubbies" for things like a glue bottle, a tape measure, or hardware, it really helps keep everything in order.

But that's not all it has to offer. Thanks to a wide, flat top and reinforced construction, the tool tote can also be used as a sturdy step stool when you need a few extra inches to get to those hard-to-reach areas.

FRONT & BACK ASSEMBLIES

The tool tote is a simple box with open cubbies to provide different storage options. Cutouts and tapers on the front and back allow easy access to all areas.

To make the tote, you can start by building two front and back assemblies. These assemblies are made up of front and back pieces with a set of legs and foot blocks added to lift the tote up off the floor. After that's all been assembled, you'll add the two tapers.

FRONT & BACK. As you can see in Figure 1, the front and back are identical. After cutting them to size from ½" plywood, I went ahead and cut the joinery. The table saw makes quick work of this.

I used a dado blade to cut the dadoes for the dividers, which are added later. Then, I switched to a regular saw blade and made a couple of passes to cut the grooves for the ¼" hardboard bottom.

MAKE THE CUTOUTS. The front and back have a wide cutout at the top to provide easy access to the main storage area. To make these cuts straight and square, I used the table saw to cut along the shorter layout lines. Then I removed the waste at the band saw and cleaned up the longer edge of the cutout with a straight bit in the router table.

ADD THE LEGS & FOOT BLOCKS. A look at Figure 2 shows how I added a second layer of plywood to the outside faces of the front and back panels. These are just pieces of ½" plywood that are glued on to form "legs." The legs raise the box off the floor, so it can be used as a convenient step stool (inset photo on previous page). And to reinforce the bottoms of the legs, I added four "foot" blocks (Figure 2).

TAPERS. The next step is to cut the tapers on the two assemblies. They soften all the sharp angles. But more importantly, they help provide easy access to the cubbies on the ends of the box. After laying out the tapers (Figure 2) cut them with a jig saw or band saw. Then, sand them smooth and square.

BEVELS. To complete the front and back assemblies, there's one last step. And that's to cut a 15° bevel on the top outside edge of the back legs (Figure 2). These bevels provide clearance when opening and closing the top. Now you can work on the dividers and ends.

1 FIGURE

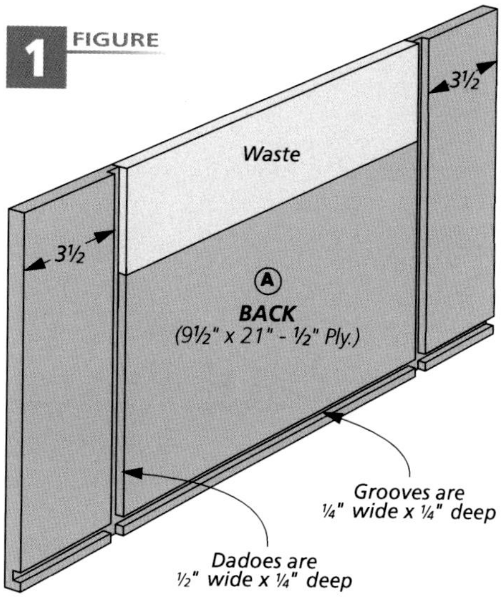

3½
Waste
3½
A
BACK
(9½" x 21" - ½" Ply.)
Grooves are ¼" wide x ¼" deep
Dadoes are ½" wide x ¼" deep

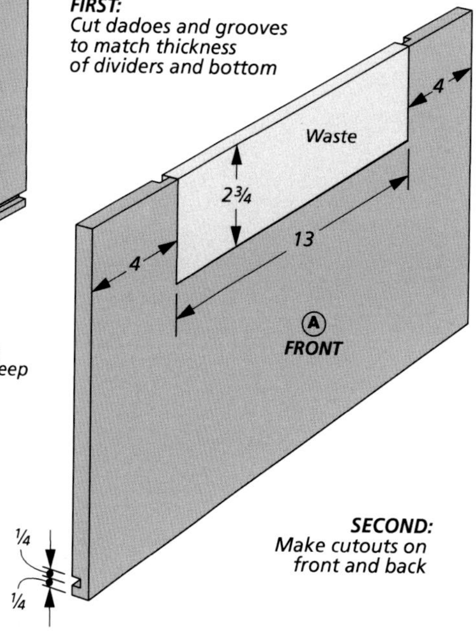

FIRST: Cut dadoes and grooves to match thickness of dividers and bottom
4
Waste
2¾
4
13
A
FRONT
¼
¼
SECOND: Make cutouts on front and back

2 FIGURE

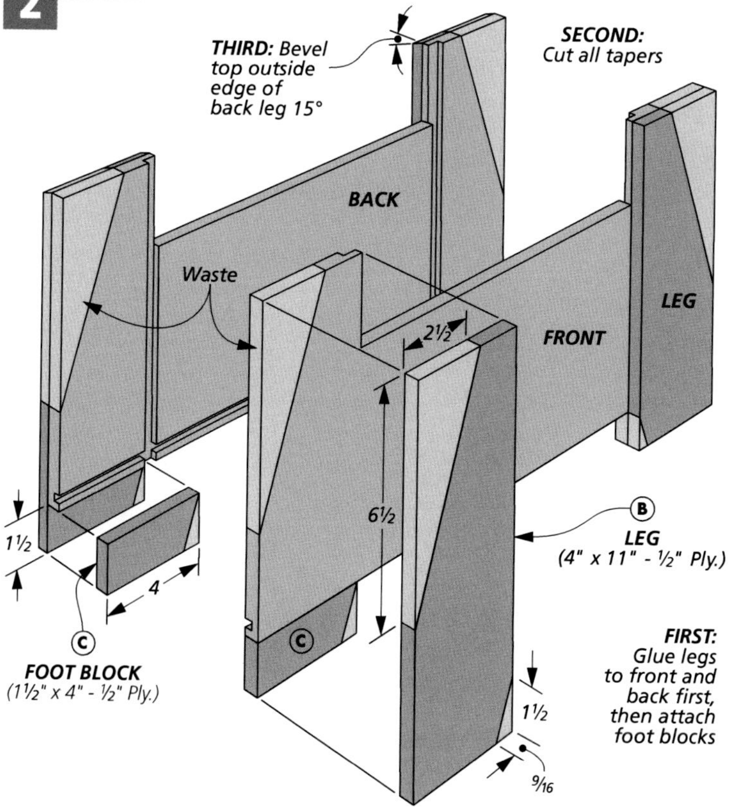

THIRD: Bevel top outside edge of back leg 15°
SECOND: Cut all tapers
BACK
Waste
LEG
2½
FRONT
6½
1½
4
C
C
FOOT BLOCK (1½" x 4" - ½" Ply.)
B
LEG (4" x 11" - ½" Ply.)
FIRST: Glue legs to front and back first, then attach foot blocks
1½
9/16

MATERIALS & SUPPLIES

A	Front/Back (2)	½ ply. - 2 x 9½
B	Legs (4)	½ ply. - 4 x 11
C	Foot Blocks (4)	½ ply. - 1½ x 4
D	Dividers (2)	½ ply. - 9 x 9
E	Cubby Ends (2)	½ ply. - 3 x 8½
F	Bottom (1)	¼ hdbd. - 9 x 20½
G	Caps (2)	¾ x 1½ - 13
H	Runners (2)	¼ x ½ - 13
I	Tray Sides (2)	⅜ x 2½ - 7⅞
J	Tray Ends (2)	⅜ x 2½ - 3⅝
K	Tray Bottom (1)	¼ hdbd. - 3⅝ x 7½
L	Top (1)	½ ply. - 11 x 16½
M	Handle Support (1)	½ x 1 - 6
N	Front Rail (1)	¾ x 2 - 12⅞
O	Back Rail (1)	¾ x 1 13/16 - 12⅞

- (1) 1½" x 13" Continuous Hinge w/Screws
- (2) 1⅝" x 2 9/16" Locking Draw Catches w/Screws

Cubbies & Cap Assembly

With the front and back assemblies completed, you're ready to finish building the rest of the tote. To do this, you'll need to make a bottom, a pair of dividers, two cubby ends, and the top.

BOTTOM & DIVIDERS. I started by cutting the ¼" hardboard bottom and ½" plywood dividers to size. The dividers fit in the dadoes you cut earlier and rest on top of the bottom, as shown in Figure 3.

CUBBY ENDS. Next, cut the cubby ends to final size from ½" plywood, adding grooves to match the ones cut earlier in the front and back. Once that's complete, it's time to assemble the main structure.

ASSEMBLY. Figure 3 gives you an idea of how the tool tote goes together. You'll glue the dividers and bottom into the dadoes and groove on the back. Then, attach the cubby ends to the bottom and back with glue, adding clamps to hold them in place. After that,

3 FIGURE

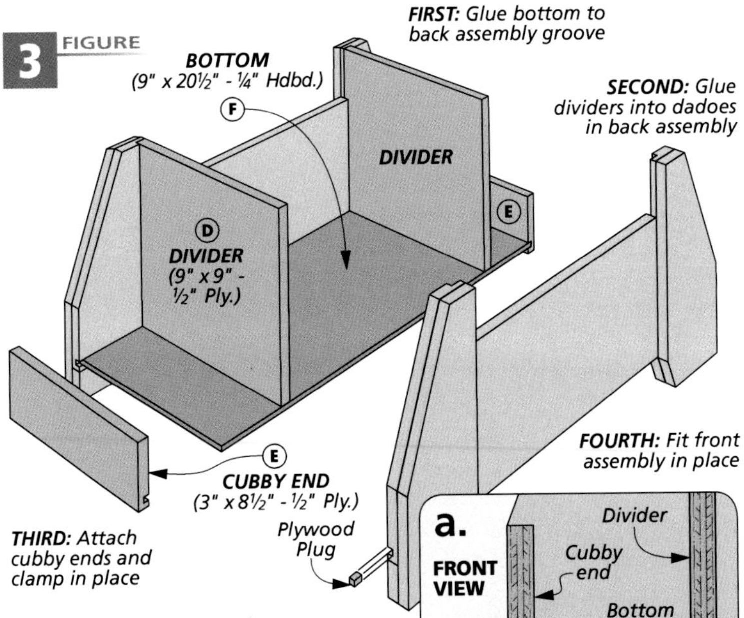

FIRST: Glue bottom to back assembly groove
BOTTOM (9" x 20½" - ¼" Hdbd.)
F
SECOND: Glue dividers into dadoes in back assembly
DIVIDER
E
D
DIVIDER (9" x 9" - ½" Ply.)
E
CUBBY END (3" x 8½" - ½" Ply.)
THIRD: Attach cubby ends and clamp in place
Plywood Plug
FOURTH: Fit front assembly in place

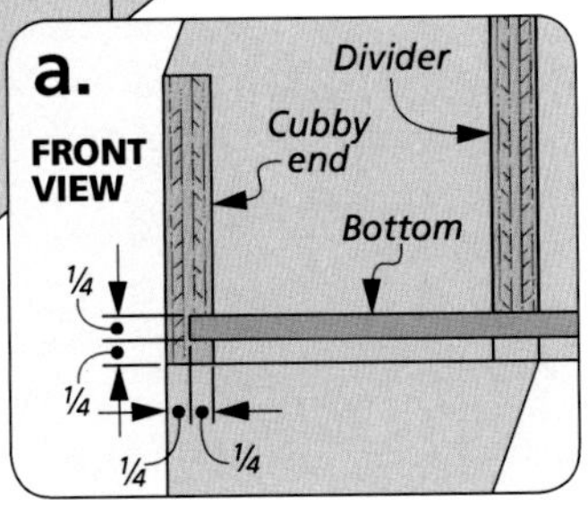

a.
FRONT VIEW
Divider
Cubby end
Bottom
¼
¼
¼
¼

all you need to do is fit the front assembly in place and clamp it up. After the glue dries, you can use pieces of scrap plywood to plug the grooves, as shown in Figure 3.

HARDWOOD CAPS & RUNNERS. The next thing you'll need to do is add a pair of ¾"-thick hardwood caps to the cutouts in the front and back assemblies. The caps hide the plywood edges and provide a solid surface for mounting the hinges and catches later. To make sure the outside face of each cap fits flush with the face of the front or back, you'll need to rabbet one edge (Figures 4 and 4b). Since the rabbet is fairly wide, cutting it on a narrow workpiece can be difficult.

A better way to do this is to start with an oversized blank. This gives you a more stable workpiece to hold on to as you make the cuts. After cutting rabbets on both sides of the blank, you can safely rip the individual caps to width.

Once the caps are cut, you can add the hardwood runners that support the tray. Then, glue the caps in place (Figure 4).

TRAY. While waiting for the glue to dry, you can build a tray to hold small items like a tape measure and pliers. It's assembled with simple tongue and dado joinery, as shown in Figures 4 and 4a. First, cut the tray ends and sides to size, then add the grooves for the ¼" hardboard bottom.

After assembling the tray with glue, rout a ⅛" chamfer around the top, outside edge. Later on, you'll see how these chamfers create a little extra room for the front rail.

4 FIGURE

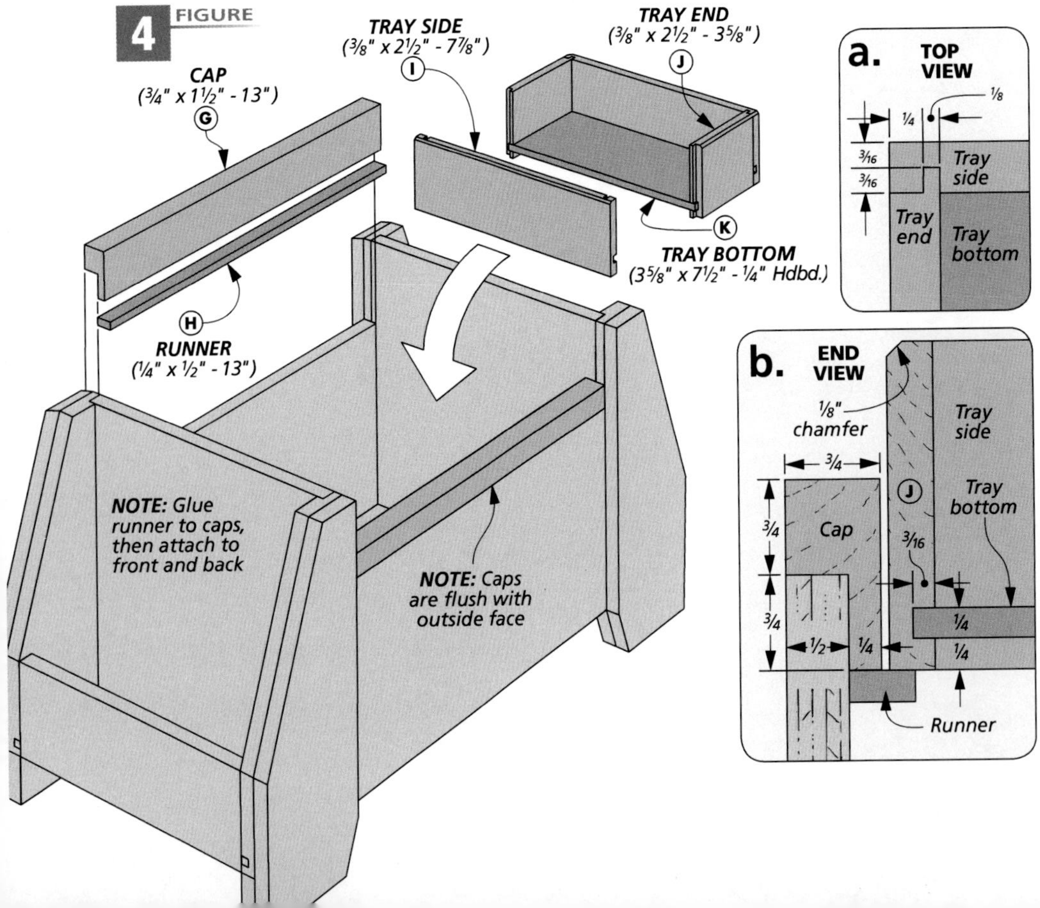

CAP (¾" x 1½" - 13")
G
TRAY SIDE (⅜" x 2½" - 7⅞")
I
TRAY END (⅜" x 2½" - 3⅝")
J
K
TRAY BOTTOM (3⅝" x 7½" - ¼" Hdbd.)
H
RUNNER (¼" x ½" - 13")
NOTE: Glue runner to caps, then attach to front and back
NOTE: Caps are flush with outside face
a. TOP VIEW
⅛
¼
³⁄₁₆
³⁄₁₆
Tray side
Tray end
Tray bottom
b. END VIEW
⅛" chamfer
¾
¾
¾
Cap
J
³⁄₁₆
Tray side
Tray bottom
½
¼
¼
¼
Runner

MAKE THE TOP

All that remains is to add the top and rails. This assembly serves three purposes. First, it allows you to keep the tools enclosed inside the tote. It also provides a place for a convenient handhold. And most importantly, by adding the rails, it acts as a sturdy step stool.

TOP. The top is cut to size from a piece of ½" plywood. Sand a small radius on each corner, and round over the top and bottom outside edges to ease all the sharp corners.

HANDHOLD. For the handhold, cut a couple of parallel slots in the top (Figure 5). Simply drill two starter holes, and then remove the waste between them with a jig saw.

To reinforce the handhold and make it more comfortable, I added a small handle support on the underside of the top. After cutting the support to size, round over the bottom edges with sandpaper. Then, glue the handle support in place on the underside of the lid, as shown in Figure 5. Finally, add

a small roundover on the top edges of the handhold slots.

RAILS. A pair of hardwood rails enclose the tool tote and reinforce the top. The first thing to do is cut the rails to size (Figure 6). You'll notice that the back rail is narrower (³⁄₁₆") than the front rail. This allows room for a continuous hinge. And the front rail has a shallow bevel on its inside edge. Along with the chamfer

on the tray, this bevel adds a little clearance so the lid will open and close with ease.

INSTALL THE RAILS. When adding the rails, the goal is to align their outside faces with the outside faces of the caps. To do this, I added the hinge first. Then, I used the dimensions given in Figures 5 and 6 to drill countersunk holes for the screws used to attach the back rail to the underside of the top.

The next step is to set the front rail on top of the cap (Figure 6). Use strips of double-sided tape to hold the rail in place. This way, the rail won't move around while you drill countersunk holes. Then, you can screw the front rail to the top.

All that's left now to complete the tool tote is to add a pair of draw catches. Once the tote is filled with tools, you can get to work on all those projects around the house you've been putting off.

5 FIGURE

TOP
(11" x 16½" - ½" Ply.)
Ⓛ

NOTE: Handle support attached to underside of lid

⅛"-rad. roundover

4³⁄₈

2¼

3

5⅛

6¾

1¼" dia.

¼"-rad. roundover

HANDLE SUPPORT
(½" x 1" - 6")
Ⓜ

a. END VIEW

1¼ — 1 — 1¼

Top

Handle support

6 FIGURE

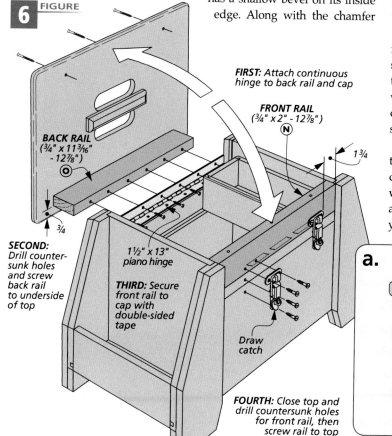

BACK RAIL
(¾" x 11³⁄₁₆" - 12⅞")
◉

SECOND: Drill countersunk holes and screw back rail to underside of top

¾

FIRST: Attach continuous hinge to back rail and cap

FRONT RAIL
(¾" x 2" - 12⅞")
Ⓝ

1¾

1½" x 13" piano hinge

THIRD: Secure front rail to cap with double-sided tape

Draw catch

FOURTH: Close top and drill countersunk holes for front rail, then screw rail to top

a. END VIEW

Tray

Continuous hinge

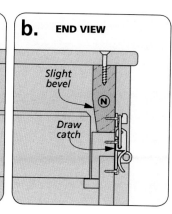

b. END VIEW

Slight bevel

Ⓝ

Draw catch

Custom
Chisel Case

Keep your chisels and other small tools close at hand and well protected in this classic, wall-mounted case.

I use my chisels on just about every project I build. So it's important for them to be easily accessible. Plus, they need to be protected so they stay sharp. The answer to both these requirements is the chisel case you see here.

The classic look isn't the only thing this case has going for it. There are a couple shelves behind the lower door to provide storage for sharpening stones, accessories, or other small tools. Plus, this case hangs on the wall, so it doesn't take up valuable benchtop space.

Finally, it's simple to build. With basic tongue and dado joinery, you'll find it goes together quickly and easily — making it the perfect way to display and protect your chisels.

Building the Case

FIGURE 1

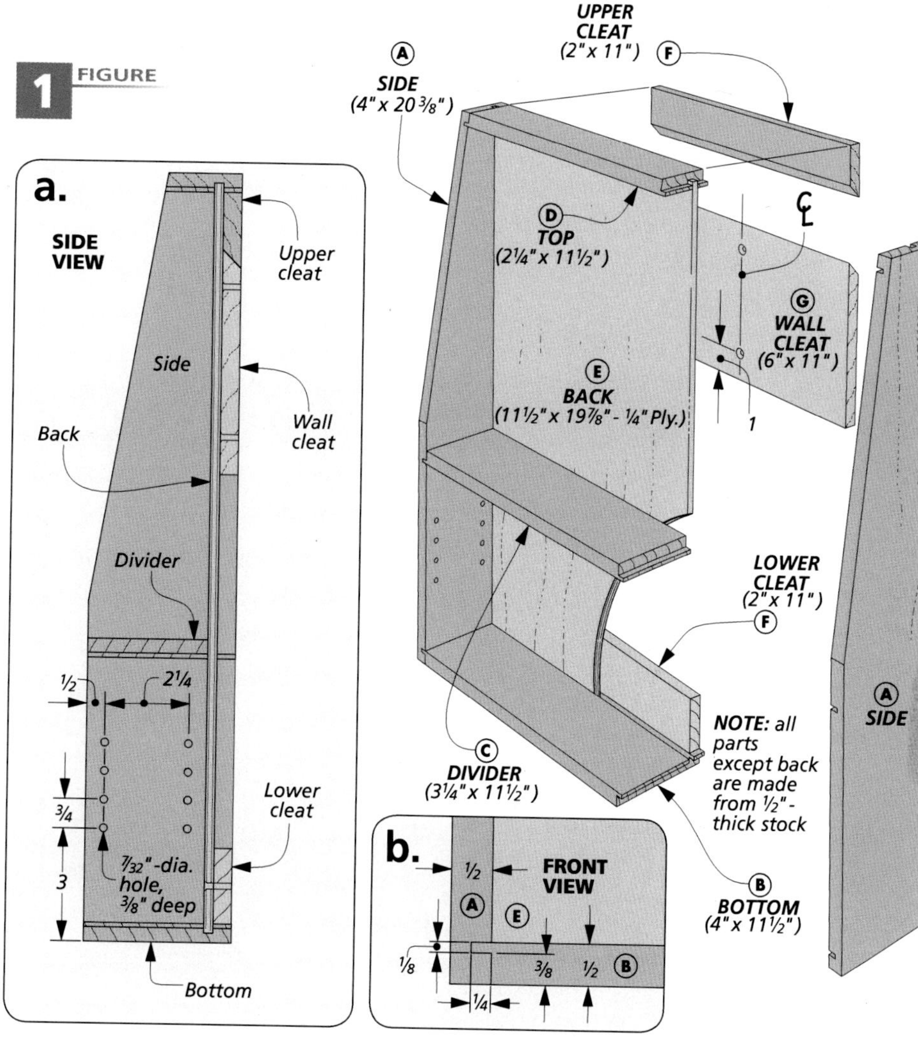

a.
SIDE VIEW
Upper cleat
Side
Wall cleat
Back
Divider
½
2¼
¾
3
Lower cleat
7⁄32"-dia. hole, ⅜" deep
Bottom
UPPER CLEAT (2"x 11")
F
A
SIDE (4"x 20⅜")
D
TOP (2¼"x 11½")
G
WALL CLEAT (6"x 11")
E
BACK (11½"x 19⅞" - ¼" Ply.)
1
LOWER CLEAT (2"x 11")
C
DIVIDER (3¼"x 11½")
NOTE: all parts except back are made from ½"-thick stock
B
BOTTOM (4"x 11½")
SIDE
b.
FRONT VIEW
⅛
⅜
¼

As I mentioned, the case is simple to build. Take a look at Figure 1. It's just a top, bottom, and divider connected to the sides with tongue and dado joinery. And a groove near the back edge of the top, bottom, and sides accepts the back. The sides are the key to the case's look, so that's where I started.

SIDES. Although the sides are tapered, it's best to complete the joinery work before shaping each one. The first step is to cut the ⅛"-wide kerfs that form the dadoes. Once that's complete, you can lay out and drill the holes for the shelf pins and then trim the sides to shape. All the information you'll need is in Figure 2. And the lower right photo shows how to smooth the sides for a perfect match.

TOP, BOTTOM & DIVIDER. At this point, you can turn your attention to the top, bottom, and divider. Here, you can start by cutting each workpiece to match the full width of each side. After the tongues are complete, you can cut the divider to final width and bevel the front edge of the top to match the sides.

To cut the tongues, I buried my dado blade in an auxiliary fence on my table saw, setting it a bit low to start with. This way, I could sneak up on the size of the tongue to create a perfect fit with the dado.

BACK. With the tongues complete, the last bit of joinery you'll need to focus on is cutting a groove for the back in the top, bottom, and sides (Figure 1a). It's sized to match the thickness of the plywood.

ASSEMBLY. Now you can cut the back to final size and assemble the case. Since the back is visible, I took the time to find a section with an attractive grain pattern and centered it on the back. I cut the door panel from the same area so it would match.

HANGING THE CASE. A pair of interlocking beveled cleats at the top create a sturdy hanging system.

Glue the upper cleat to the back of the case, and screw the wide mating cleat to the wall later. To ensure the case won't "pop out" from the wall while opening the door, screw through the lower cleat to fix the case to the wall.

Cutting the Sides. After cutting the tapered sides at the band saw, clamp the two pieces together and sand them smooth with a sanding block.

FIGURE 2

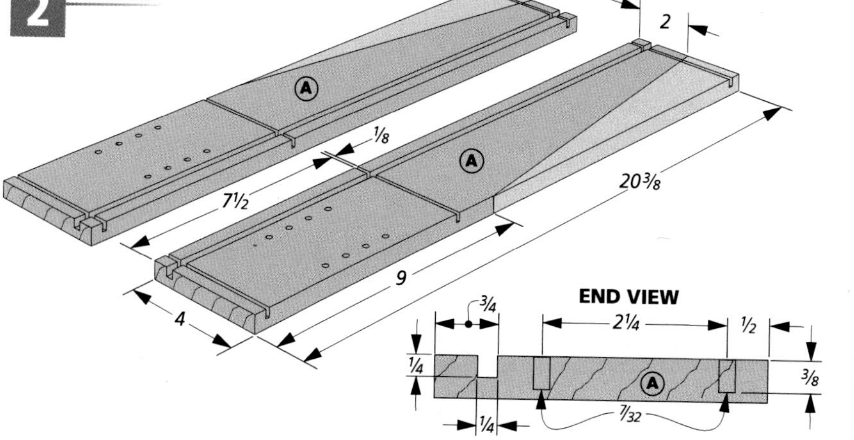

A
2
⅛
7½
20⅜
9
4
END VIEW
¾
2¼
½
¼
⅜
7⁄32

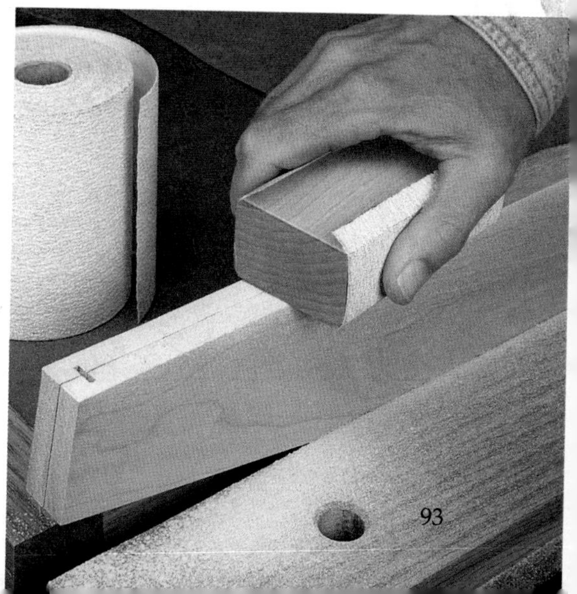

Outfitting the **Case**

Now that you've completed the basic case, the next few steps will add some decorative details, a rack for the chisels, and a door.

CAP & BASE. To complement the classic looks of the case, I added a beveled cap and base, as you see in Figure 3. The nice thing about them is they're pretty straightforward to make. After cutting them to final size, all you need to do is tilt the saw blade and knock off the front edge and ends at the top of the base and bottom of the cap.

With the bevels cut, the next step is to glue the cap and base in place. While this face-to-face glue-up provides a lot of strength, the slippery glue makes it a challenge to keep the parts from shifting out of place.

To keep the workpieces right where they need to be, I tapped in a couple of small brads and then clipped off the heads, leaving a sharp end. Then as you clamp the cap and base down, you don't need to worry about them shifting.

ADD THE TRIM. The door that's added later will cover up the lower part of the case joinery. But to cover the exposed joint at the top of the case, you'll have to add a thin piece of trim. Since the trim needs to match the angle of the sides (10°), make the cut on an oversized workpiece first. Then, cut it to final size and glue it in place.

3 FIGURE

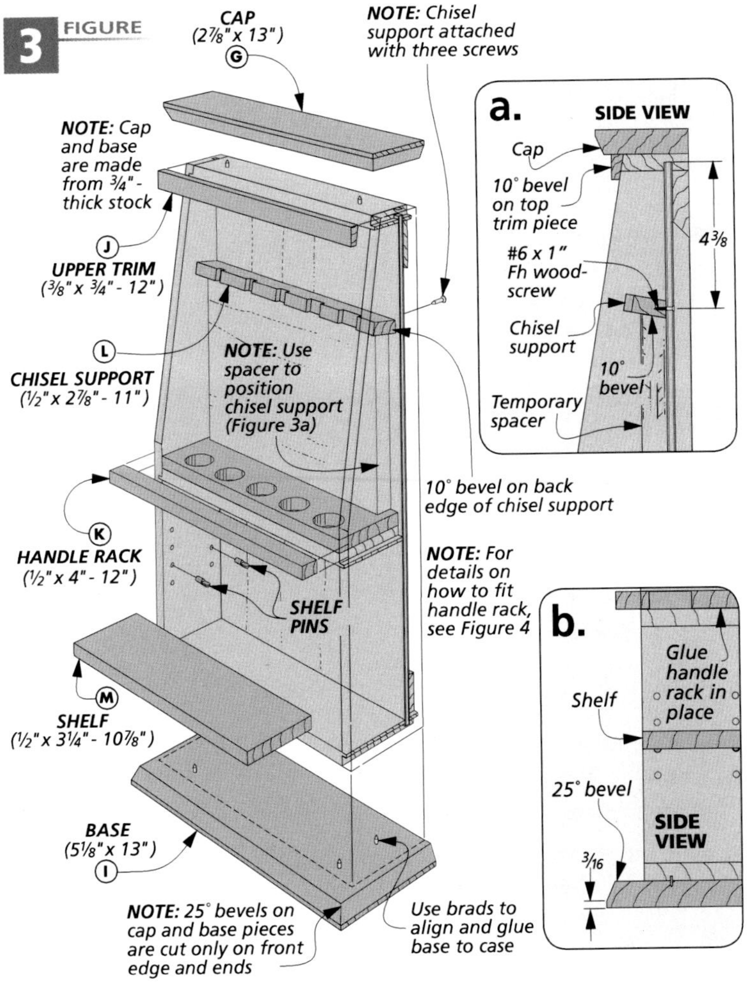

CAP
(2⅞" x 13")
G
NOTE: Chisel support attached with three screws
NOTE: Cap and base are made from ¾"-thick stock
J
UPPER TRIM
(⅜" x ¾" - 12")
L
CHISEL SUPPORT
(½" x 2⅞" - 11")
NOTE: Use spacer to position chisel support (Figure 3a)
10° bevel on back edge of chisel support
K
HANDLE RACK
(½" x 4" - 12")
SHELF PINS
NOTE: For details on how to fit handle rack, see Figure 4
M
SHELF
(½" x 3¼" - 10⅞")
BASE
(5⅛" x 13")
I
NOTE: 25° bevels on cap and base pieces are cut only on front edge and ends
Use brads to align and glue base to case
a.
SIDE VIEW
Cap
10° bevel on top trim piece
#6 x 1" Fh woodscrew
4⅜
Chisel support
10° bevel
Temporary spacer
b.
Glue handle rack in place
Shelf
25° bevel
SIDE VIEW
3⁄16

CHISEL RACK. With that complete, the next step is to provide a way to keep chisels stored securely, yet easily accessible. To do this, add the handle rack and support in Figure 4.

But there's a challenge to this. The handle rack needs to fit in place without any gaps at the ends, back, or where it meets the

4 FIGURE

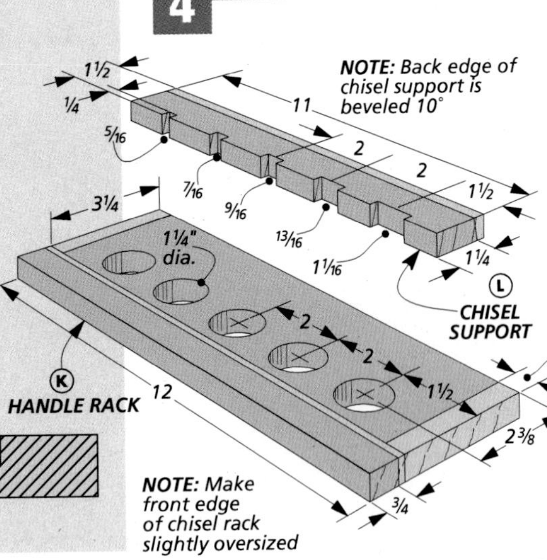

1½
¼
11
NOTE: Back edge of chisel support is beveled 10°
5⁄16
2
2
7⁄16
9⁄16
1½
3¼
13⁄16
1¼" dia.
1 1⁄16
1¼
L
CHISEL SUPPORT
2
2
1½
K
HANDLE RACK
12
2⅜
¾
NOTE: Make front edge of chisel rack slightly oversized

MATERIALS, SUPPLIES & CUTTING DIAGRAM

A	Sides (2)	½ x 4 - 20⅜
B	Bottom (1)	½ x 4 - 11½
C	Middle Panel (1)	½ x 3¼ - 11½
D	Case Top (1)	½ x 2¼ - 11½
E	Back Panel (1)	¼ ply. - 11½ x 19⅞
F	Cabinet Cleats (2)	¾ x 2 - 11
G	Wall Cleat (1)	¾ x 6 - 11
H	Cap (1)	¾ x 2⅞ - 13
I	Base (1)	¾ x 5⅛ - 13
J	Upper Trim (1)	⅜ x ¾ - 12
K	Handle Rack (1)	½ x 4 - 12
L	Chisel Support (1)	½ x 2⅞ - 11
M	Shelf (1)	½ x 3¼ - 10⅞
N	Door Stiles (2)	½ x 1 - 7⅞
O	Door Rails (2)	½ x 1 - 10½
P	Door Panel (1)	¼ ply. - 6⅜ x 10½

- (1 pr.) 2" No-Mortise Hinges
- (1) 16mm Brass Knob w/screw
- (4) 5mm Pin Supports
- (1) ¼" Rare Earth Magnet
- (1) ⅜" Magnet Cup
- (1) ⅜" Strike Washer
- (1) #4 x ⅜" Fh Woodscrew
- (2) #6 x 1" Fh Woodscrew

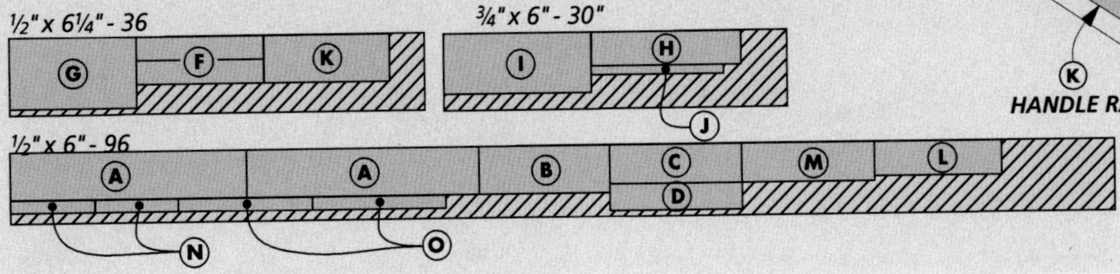

½" x 6¼" - 36
G
F
K
¾" x 6" - 30"
I
H
J
½" x 6" - 96
A
A
B
C
D
M
L
N
O

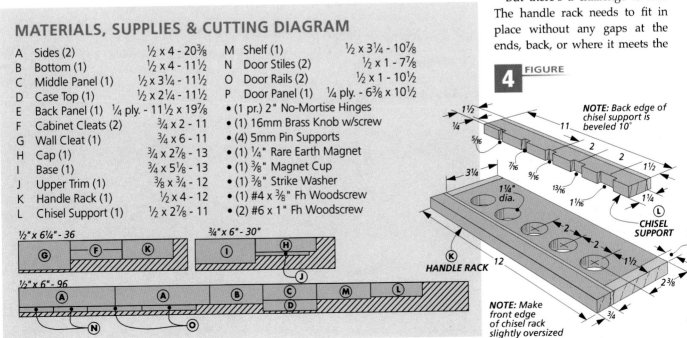

front edge of each side. Since there wasn't really an easy way to sneak up on the fit, I made the handle rack in two pieces, as illustrated in the lower part of Figure 4.

To do this, I started by cutting an extra-wide blank that matched the overall width of the case. Then, I trimmed a narrow strip off the front edge (Figure 4).

Now, trim the larger piece to fit the opening between the sides, cutting a little off each end. (This helps keep the grain matched up with the narrow strip you just cut off.)

Once you have a good fit, all you need to do is glue the two parts back together to create the rack. Just be sure to carefully glue them in place so the notch at each end is sized identically. The rack still needs to be cut to final width, so simply trim the back edge until it slips into place flush at the back and front edge of the sides.

To complete the handle rack, all that's left to do is to drill holes for the handle of each chisel. Then you can glue the rack in place.

CHISEL SUPPORT. The handle rack keeps the chisels in place at the bottom. But to corral them at the top, you'll add a notched chisel support, like you see in Figure 4.

The only tricky part here is locating the support properly. To do this,

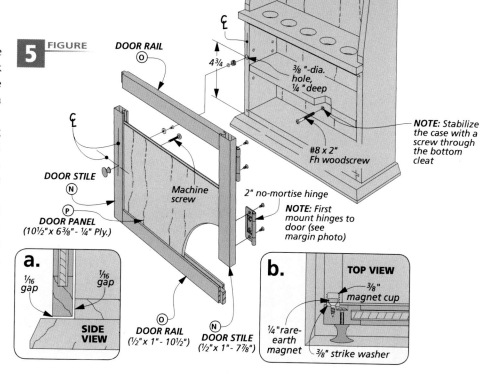

5 FIGURE

DOOR RAIL (O)

4¾"

⅜"-dia. hole, ¼" deep

NOTE: Stabilize the case with a screw through the bottom cleat

#8 x 2" Fh woodscrew

DOOR STILE (N)
(P)
DOOR PANEL (10½" x 6⅜" - ¼" Ply.)

Machine screw

2" no-mortise hinge

NOTE: First mount hinges to door (see margin photo)

a.
1/16 gap
1/16 gap
SIDE VIEW

DOOR RAIL (O) (½" x 1" - 10½")

DOOR STILE (N) (½" x 1" - 7⅞")

b. TOP VIEW
⅜" magnet cup
¼" rare-earth magnet
⅜" strike washer

I cut a beveled spacer from ¾" plywood and laid it against the back as a guide, as in Figure 3a.

THE DOOR. To complete the case, you just need to add a door. A frame and panel door maintains a classic look and mounts to the case with a pair of no-mortise hinges.

The box below shows how to make the stub tenons and grooves used on the door. When sizing the parts, be sure that the door matches the width of the case and that there's a 1/16" gap at the top and bottom, like you see in Figure 5a.

MOUNT THE DOOR. Once the door is completed, you're about ready to mount it to the case. But to match the gap that will be created by the hinge, you'll need to fit a washer into a counterbore drilled in the back of the door (Figure 5b).

After adding the magnet to the case and the knob to the door, you can mount the door to the case. Then, simply cut a shelf to size and screw the case to the wall.

With this classic case near your workbench, you'll be able to find a sharp chisel whenever you need it.

No-Mortise Hinges. Hinges are mounted ⅝" from the top and bottom of the door.

Stub Tenon & Groove Joinery

Frame & Panel Door. The door is constructed using stub tenon and groove joinery.

Making a frame and panel door on the table saw takes just a few steps.

After you have the stiles and rails cut to length, you'll have to cut a groove to match the thickness of the plywood. An easy way to do this is to make two passes — flipping the workpiece between passes, as you see in the upper drawing and detail at right.

To cut the tenons on the ends of the rails, use a dado blade buried in an auxiliary fence, as shown in the lower drawing. Start with the blade set low and sneak up on the fit (lower detail).

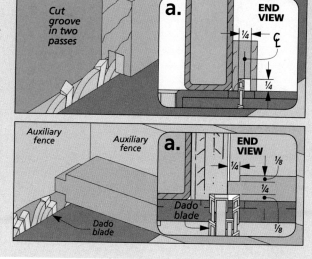

Cut groove in two passes

a. END VIEW
¼
¼

Auxiliary fence
Auxiliary fence
a. END VIEW
¼
⅛
¼
Dado blade
Dado blade
⅛

Router Bit
Storage

Keep your router bits and accessories front and center with this easy-to-build weekend project.

For the longest time, it wasn't unusual to find router bits (and other router accessories) tucked away in every corner of my shop. Finally, after I spent more time looking for a router bit than actually using it, I knew it was time to get organized. The storage center you see at left was the solution. It keeps all my bits and accessories in one spot, protected, and right at hand.

SMALL PROJECT, BIG FEATURES. The storage center has a number of handy features. For starters, there are three removable shelves for storing router bits. You can slip out a shelf and take it right where you need to work — whether that's at a router table, like you see in the photo at left, or across the shop at your workbench (with a hand-held router).

To ensure that you'll be able to store just about any size or shape router bit, there are two different shelf designs. The drawings on the opposite page show the hole arrangements I used. But you can make whatever combination of shelves, holes, and patterns you need to suit your own collection of router bits.

Finally, you don't want to lose track of all your router odds and ends, like wrenches and collets. That's

Removable Shelves. The shelves can be customized to suit your set of router bits. And each shelf slides in and out with ease, so you can take it right where you need it.

CONSTRUCTION DETAILS

OVERALL DIMENSIONS:
28" H x 16" W x 4 3/8" D

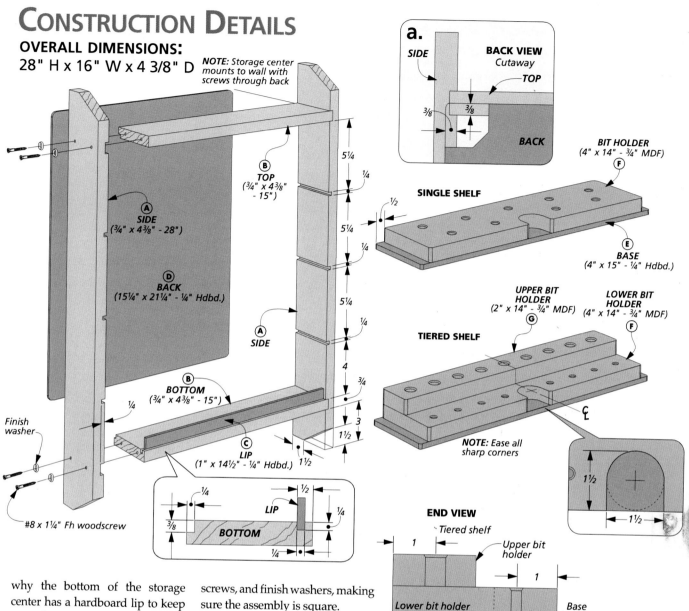

NOTE: Storage center mounts to wall with screws through back

a.

SIDE

BACK VIEW
Cutaway

TOP

3/8   3/8

BACK

SINGLE SHELF

1/2

BIT HOLDER
(4" x 14" - 3/4" MDF)
F

BASE
(4" x 15" - 1/4" Hdbd.)
E

B
TOP
(3/4" x 4 3/8" - 15")

5 1/4

1/4

5 1/4

1/4

A
SIDE
(3/4" x 4 3/8" - 28")

D
BACK
(15 1/4" x 21 1/4" - 1/4" Hdbd.)

5 1/4

1/4

A
SIDE

UPPER BIT HOLDER
(2" x 14" - 3/4" MDF)
G

LOWER BIT HOLDER
(4" x 14" - 3/4" MDF)
F

TIERED SHELF

4

3/4

B
BOTTOM
(3/4" x 4 3/8" - 15")

Finish washer

1/4

C
LIP
(1" x 14 1/2" - 1/4" Hdbd.)

3

1 1/2

1 1/2

NOTE: Ease all sharp corners

C

1 1/2

1 1/2

#8 x 1 1/4" Fh woodscrew

1/4   1/2

LIP

1/4

3/8   **BOTTOM**

1/4

END VIEW

Tiered shelf

1   *Upper bit holder*

1

Lower bit holder   Base

---

why the bottom of the storage center has a hardboard lip to keep everything neatly contained.

MAKE THE FRAME. I started on the storage center by making a hardwood frame. As you can see in the drawing above, it's nothing more than a pair of sides, along with a top and bottom. Dadoes cut at each end of the sides are sized to match the top and bottom. And a set of narrower dadoes (1/4") will hold the shelves you'll make later.

Once all the dadoes are complete, you can knock off the top and bottom corners of the sides to ease the sharp edges. Then, cut a groove along the front edge of the bottom piece to accept the hardboard lip.

With the joinery complete, you can assemble the frame with glue,

screws, and finish washers, making sure the assembly is square.

To keep the frame from racking, add a 1/4" hardboard back. As you can see in detail 'a,' you'll need to rout a rabbet along the inside back edge of the frame. After cutting the back to size, round off the corners and glue the back in place.

SHELVES. At this point, you're ready to make the shelves that hold the bits. Each shelf is simply a 1/4" hardboard base with a single or double layer of MDF making up each bit holder.

But before you start cutting the shelves to size or drilling any holes, get all your router bits together. This way, you can use the drawings above and your personal collection of router bits to determine

the best way to customize a set of shelves to suit your needs.

Once you have the holes laid out, drill them slightly oversized (1/32"). Then, chamfer the top edge so the shanks slip in and out easily (or simply sand the holes a bit after drilling them out). Before gluing the bit holders to the base, cut a centered notch to provide a convenient way to pull the shelf out (lower photo on opposite page).

FILL IT UP. To mount the storage center to the wall, simply screw through the back. Finally, you can fill the storage center with all your router bits and accessories.

Weekend Woodworking **Sources**

MAIL ORDER SOURCES

Rockler
800-279-4441
rockler.com

amazon.com

General Finishes
800-783-6050
generalfinishes.com

Horton Brasses
800-754-9127
horton-brasses.com

Lee Valley
800-871-8158
leevalley.com

The Webstaurant Store
717-392-7472
webstaurantstore.com

Woodworker's Supply
800-645-9292
woodworker.com

ZAR
570-344-1202
ugl.com

DVD STORAGE CASE

The only hardware you'll need to build the DVD storage case on page 12 is brass file drawer pulls with cardholders (70763) and stem bumper glides (28373) to help the drawer slide easily. And if you plan on making more than one storage case and connecting them, you'll also need $\frac{1}{4}$"-20 standard barbed threaded inserts (31872) and $\frac{1}{4}$" x 1" Fh machine screws. All of these items are available from *Rockler*.

DROP-FRONT STORAGE

The storage center on page 18 looks great, and it doesn't take a lot of material to build. The hardware you'll need for the project includes double coat hooks (00W80.01) from *Lee Valley* and $1\frac{1}{4}$"-dia. maple knobs (WK-6) and drop-leaf table hinges (H-505) from *Horton Brasses*. You'll also need a $\frac{3}{8}$"-dia. rare-earth magnet (32907) and washer from *Rockler*.

PANELED WINDOW SEAT

The pre-made pieces for the paneled window seat on page 28 are pretty common styles (colonial baseboard, panel molding, and beadboard), but they may vary slightly from store to store. It's not critical that the moldings you use precisely match those shown. If necessary, you can make minor adjustments to the design.

DESK CLOCK

The most important piece of hardware you'll need to build the desk clock on page 36 is a $3\frac{1}{2}$"-dia. quartz, "press-in" clock movement. (The movement I used is available from *Woodworker's Supply*.) To create the 3"-dia. opening for the body of the movement, *Lee Valley* offers a 3" saw-tooth bit (06J01.48). Then, you just need posterboard and adhesive-backed felt to line the compartment.

DESKTOP MESSAGE CENTER

The brass hinges for the message center on page 44 can be ordered from *Lee Valley* (00D01.01). And the spring you need for the pop-up note dispenser is a $\frac{3}{4}$"-long (free length) closed-end compression spring, 0.48" in diameter. The most important dimension to remember for the spring is its free length (not compressed).

COUNTERTOP CONTAINERS

For the kitchen containers on page 62, you need nickel-plated case hinges (00S55.01) from *Lee Valley*. However, the screws that come with those hinges are too long. You need to order $\frac{1}{2}$"-long screws. You also need approximately 1,600 10" bamboo skewers for the knife box. I found them online at *The Webstaurant Store*. The boxes are finished with a wipe-on varnish.

POT RACK

The hanger rod (01W83.19), shelf supports (00S06.52), and stainless steel S-hooks (12K34.22) for the kitchen pot rack on page 66 can be purchased from *Lee Valley*. The finish is *ZAR* cherry stain.

SERVING TRAY

No hardware is needed to build the serving tray on page 70. But I did add decorative window film to the acrylic tray bottom. There are a variety of designs available from *Amazon*.

CUTTING BOARDS

I finished the cutting boards on page 74 with *General Finishes' Salad Bowl Finish*. It's available through *Rockler*.

CHISEL CABINET

All the hardware for the chisel cabinet on page 92 is available through *Lee Valley*. Here are the part numbers: 2" no-mortise hinge (00H51.22), 16mm brass knob (01A02.16), 5mm pin supports (00S10.05), $\frac{1}{4}$" rare-earth magnet (99K31.01), $\frac{3}{8}$" magnet cup (99K32.51), $\frac{3}{8}$" strike washer (99K32.61), and #4 x $\frac{3}{8}$" Fh woodscrews (91Z04.02).

Made in the USA
Middletown, DE
09 October 2024

62293307R00055